Published by Aperitifs Publishing Company
Santa Rosa, California
707-523-1611
johncburton@msn.com

ISBN-13: 978-0-692-88232-0
Library of Congress Control Number: 2017906634

Copyright © May 2017 John C. Burton

Written by John C. Burton

Merle Avila's tokens referenced to Charles Kappen's guide books

Additional information provided by John Louder

Majority of bottles referenced in Burton collection

Additional bottle photos referenced to Richard & Rick Siri

Printed in the United States of America

All rights reserved. No part of this book may be reproduced or transformed in any form or by any means, electronic or mechanical, including photocopying, recording, or by any information storage and/or retrieval system without permission in writing from the authors or publisher.

Every attempt has been made to provide accurate information on the following subjects.

The first checklist of Sonoma County bottles, **EARLY BOTTLES OF SONOMA COUNTY** was published by the Northwestern Bottle Collectors Association in 1973 edited by Frank Sternad. The publication was followed up by **EARLY BOTTLES OF MARIN COUNTY** edited by George Epperson with contributions by Eric McGuire and Barbara Coggins. Both editions were excellent references of the day.

I have been more fortunate than Frank and George because of the computer which allows me to cut, paste, and insertion of photos. This book is as complete as I know it to be because there will always be new finds, variations and the person who may have an item that won't participate for whatever reasons.

Special thanks go to NBCA club president Merle Avila for sharing his tremendous token collection that represents the bars, saloons and cigar stores featured in this publication. Thanks to Richard Siri and Rick Siri for allowing me to photograph a few of their bottles and to John Louder for his research.

This book will be followed up with a catalog of Sonoma County proprietary drug store medicine bottles.

BOTTLES, TOKENS, BEER CANS & HISTORY
OF
SONOMA COUNTY

Bottles, Tokens and History of Sonoma County are a work compiled by John C. Burton, and Merle Avila who are members of the Northwestern Bottle Collectors Association in Sonoma County, California.

We have compiled information regarding soda bottlers, beer bottlers and brewers, saloons and their advertising trade tokens. As with all reference books this is a work in progress as new information always seems to appear after it is "finished" and published.

John C. Burton has been a collector of Sonoma County bottles, beer cans and memorabilia and a member of the Northwestern Bottle Collector's Association (NBCA) since 1978. As a past-president and current secretary of the club he has published much information of the enclosed content in this publication. A member of the 49er Chapter of the Beer Can Collectors of America (BCCA) and is an authority of Grace Brothers Brewery, Santa Rosa.

Merle Avila has brought a wealth of information to our club and publication through his extensive token collection. As president of the NBCA, his valuable skills and leadership has been a driving force that has made our meetings more interesting and valuable to our membership. He is also president of the Sonoma County Coin club, president of the Western States Token Association and past president and current vice-president of National Token Association.

John Louder has proved invaluable in research and providing information for this publication. He has spent numerous hours at the Sonoma County Library History Annex and Sonoma County Recorder's Office gathering information that has assisted in making this publication more interesting and correct.

John started collection at the young age of 4 or 5 years while playing in the dirt at the old house on Stewart Street here in Santa Rosa. He would occasionally find a marble or an army soldier from which he enjoyed finding something old in the dirt. His mother told him "that must have belonged to a little boy who lived here a long time ago." Being curious he questioned "Who was that kid and what became of him?" Today, it's no different, "Who were these people and what became of them."

A special thanks to Richard and Rick Siri for providing additional photos of bottles.

We close with a special thank you to both Lou & Leisa Lambert who have been the couple that have continued to make our bottle show a success the first week of May every year. Go on-line to WWW.OLDWESTBOTTLES.COM and click on "Shows" for more information regarding our club.

ACKNOWLEDGMENTS

The first checklist of Sonoma County bottles, **EARLY BOTTLES OF SONOMA COUNTY** was published by the Northwestern Bottle Collectors Association (NBCA) in 1973 edited by Frank Sternad and has been the illustrated descriptive guide and check list of Sonoma County bottles available to collectors.

Well, 44 years later we decided to update that publication and include photos of Sonoma County soda, and whiskey bottles as well as Grace Bros. beer cans. We have also included saloon and trade tokens that match the bottles. These tokens were issued to stimulate trade bringing back the customers.

That publication was followed by **EARLY BOTTLES OF MARIN COUNTY** edited by George Epperson with contributions by Eric McGuire and Barbara Coggins. Both editions were excellent references of the day.

I have been more fortunate than Frank and George because of the computer which allows me to cut, paste, and insertion of photos. This book is as complete as I know it to be because there will always be new finds, variations and the person who may have an item that won't participate for whatever reasons.

The majority of bottles shown in this book are from the collection of John C. Burton with additions from Merle Avila, John Louder, Richard Siri and Rick Siri.

Our special thanks go to club member John Louder who has spent tireless research at the Sonoma County Historical Annex in Santa Rosa Louder for his invaluable assistance in researching the Press Democrat and finding articles that I missed and to Katherine J. Rinehart, M. A. History and Genealogy Library Manager. Both have been of great assistance in helping complete this publication.

And thank you to NBCA club president Merle Avila for sharing his tremendous token collection that represents the bars, saloons and cigar stores featured in this publication. All of the tokens featured in this book are from his collection. The amount of time he spent photographing these tokens was incredible. All token listings are referenced to Charles Kappen's token books.

TABLE OF CONTENTS

Acknowledgements …………………………………………………	i
Table of Contents ………………………………………………………	ii
Views of Lou & Leisa Lambert, Master Diggers ………………	vi
Burton & Daughter Kelley Hunter – Avila & Everett Liljeberg……….	viii
Members McGuire, Siri's, Ritz Ingraham & Ingle…………..………	ix

INTRODUCTION

Bottling Companies …………………………………………………	Page 1
Bottle Archaeology …………………………………………………	Page 2
Building a Collection ………………………………………………	Page 3
Clubs & Organizations ……………………………………………	Page 4
Beer Cans & Go-Withs ……………………………………………	Page 5
Values, New Finds, Reproductions & Fakes ……………………	Page 6

SODA BOTTLES, BREWERS AND BOTTLERS

Boyes Hot Springs ………………………………………	Page 7
Healdsburg, F. O. Brandt ………………………………………	Page 10
Healdsburg, White Star Saloon ……………………………………..	Page 13
Lytton Springs ………………………………………	Page 18
Occidental Bert Philbrick ………………………………………	Page 19
Petaluma, B. F. Connolly by Fred Leoni……………………………	Page 20
Petaluma, John Endres ………………………………………	Page 22
Petaluma, Capitol Bottling Works by Ed Mannion ……………………	Page 23
Petaluma, Capitol Bottling Works, Louis Schmidt………………..	Page 25
Petaluma, Capitol Bottling Works, Hammerman & Jarr …………..	Page 26
Petaluma Soda Works, Klammer & Malz …………………………	Page 27
Petaluma Soda Works, Hammerlind & Larson ………………………	Page 28
Petaluma Brewery Christlich, Efinger, Blatz & Schierhold …………	Page 30
Petaluma Brewery Robuson, Fischer, Gerckens, Mellitzer & Grace…	Page 32
Petaluma Eagle Brewing Company Thomas G. Edwards ……………	Page 33
Sonoma Brewery of Petaluma, Mitchell & George Griess ……………	Page 34
Petaluma United States Brewery George Griess ………………………	Page 35
Preston, Barcal, John Kolling ………………………………………	Page 36
Santa Rosa, IXL, Stollar Brothers …………………………………	Page 39
Santa Rosa, Gilt Edge, George Szameitat & Jacob Joost ...…………	Page 40
Santa Rosa, Rose City Soda Works, Mathews & Roberts ……………	Page 41
Santa Rosa Rose City Soda Works Elmer Brown ………………………	Page 43
Santa Rosa, T & H Bottling Company ………………………………	Page 44
Santa Rosa, P. J. Sullivan Soda Works ………………………………	Page 45
Santa Rosa Soda Works Chronological Order ………………………	Page 46
Santa Rosa Soda Works, Hudson & Palmer ……..…………………	Page 49
Santa Rosa Soda Works, Albert Callori ………………………………..	Page 55

TABLE OF CONTENTS

Hudson Purchases Cigar Store …………………………………………	Page 56
Hudson Purchases First & Last Chance Saloon ……………………	Page 57
Hudson Purchases Old Corner Saloon & Loses License ………………	Page 58
Santa Rosa, Grace Brothers Bottles…………………………………	Page 59
Santa Rosa Grace Brothers Paper Labels…………………………..	Page 65
Santa Rosa Grace Brothers Beer Cans ……………………………..	Page 69
Santa Rosa, James Brucker Soda Works & Weiland's Beer …………	Page 80
Santa Rosa, Sam Alexander Roseland ……………………………	Page 81
Santa Rosa Budola Sparkling Beverage …………………………..	Page 82
Sebastopol Bottling Works Chronological Order ……………………..	Page 83
Sebastopol, Zimmerman Brothers, Enterprise Bottling ………………	Page 84
Sebastopol, Crystal Bottling Works & George Sollars Bottling ………	Page 85
Sebastopol Sollars Secures Coca Cola Contract ……………………..Page 86
Sebastopol Kist Bottling Company ………………………………....	Page 87
Sonoma Brewing Company …………………………………………Page 88
Sonoma Brewing Company Incorporation ……………………………..	Page 89
Sonoma Valley Soda Works ………………………………………..	Page 90

WHISKEY BOTTLES & RELATED TOKENS
SANTA ROSA

Boulevard………………………………………………………..	Page 93
Capitol Saloon ………………………………………………………....	Page 94
Castle Saloon ……………………………………………………..	Page 95
Club Saloon ………………………………………………………	Page 98
Commercial Headquarters ………………………………………	Page 99
Cub Billiard & Pool Parlor ………………………………………….Page 100
Germania Hotel ……………………………………………………..	Page 101
Grape Vine Saloon …………………………………………………..	Page 103
Grand Hotel ………………………………………………………..	Page 107
Hotel La Rose …………………………………………………….	Page 110
Hotel Torino ………………………………………………………	Page 111
Humboldt Saloon …………………………………………………..	Page 112
Jack's Club …………………………………………………………	Page 113
J. M. Roney ………………………………………………………..	Page 114
Jones & Mathews Saloon …………………………………………..	Page 118
Lodge Saloon ……………………………………………………….	Page 120
Milano Saloon (U. S. Saloon) ……………………………………….	Page 121
New Corner Saloon ……………………………………………………Page 123
Northwestern Liquor Store (Gemetti's) ……………………………..	Page 124
Occidental Hotel ………………………………………………….	Page 135
Old Corner Saloon ………………………………………………..	Page 137

TABLE OF CONTENTS

O. K. Saloon	Page 138
Palace Liquor Saloon	Page 139
Peerless Saloon	Page 141
Royal Saloon, Quinlan & Jesse W. Daw	Page 143
Sample Room	Page 145
Santa Rosa House	Page 146
Second Class Saloon	Page 147
Senate Saloon	Page 148
The Model Saloon	Page 150
The Oberon	Page 155
The Reception	Page 161
The Tavern	Page 162
The Welcome Saloon	Page 163
The When (AKA the Recall)	Page 166
The Windsor Saloon	Page 167
The Wrenn	Page 168
Toscano Hotel	Page 169
Western Hotel	Page 171

CLOVERDALE

Frank Spencer Saloon	Page 175
U-Auto Bar (Mitchel Bros.) & U. S. Hotel	Page 176
Gibson Saloon & Palace Saloon	Page 177

HEALDSBURG

Wine Creek Vineyards	Page 178
Owl Hollow, Massoni & Fava	Page 179

PETALUMA

Keller's Bar	Page 180
P. Morville's Whiskey	Page 181

SEBASTOPOL

Speas Brandy Distillery	Page 182
Speas Apple Jack	Page 183
Sebastopol Big Deal Winery	Page 185

ISAAC DeTURK – LACHMAN & JACOBI

Santa Rosa, I. De Turk Lithograph & Bottles	Page 186
Santa Rosa, De Turk Wine & Brandy Bottles	Page 187
De Turk Pocket Knife	Page 191

Kopf & Donovan .... Page 192
Petaluma, Lachman & Jacobi Wine & Port Bottles .... Page 195

SANTA ROSA CIGAR STORE TOKENS

I. W. Bernstein ……………………………………………… Page 199
Kurlander's ………………………………………………… Page 200
La Brazoria Cigar Store (Bower & Mercier) …………………….Page 201
Mac Killop Brothers Cigars …………………………............ …………Page 202
Muther Cigars …………………………………………… Page 203
Indian Cigar Store………………………………………… Page 204
Ramsey Cigar Store ……………………………………….Page 205
Walter Schmid Cigars …………………………………….Page 206
George W. Wells Cigars ………………………………….. Page 207
F. M. Wilson Cigars - The Past Time Cigar Stand …………….… Page 208

**DEDICATED TO MEMBERS OF THE
ANTIQUE BOTTLE COLLECTING FRATERNITY**

Where do the majority of new bottle finds come from?

NWBCA club member Lou Lambert

**DEDICATED TO MEMBERS OF THE
ANTIQUE BOTTLE COLLECTING FRATERNITY**

NWBCA club member Leisa Lambert

**No, this doesn't happen with every dig.
For more information:
nbca@comcast.net**

SANTA ROSA ANTIQUE BOTTLE SHOW

**For show dates and more information go on-line to
nbca@comcast.net
Or
http://oldwestbottles.com/SantaRosaShow.php**

**Left: John C. Burton with daughter Kelley Burton-Hunter
Right: Merle Avila with Santa Rosa Club Member Everett Liljeberg**

Santa Rosa Club Members

Richard Siri – Eric McGuire – Rick Siri **Frank Ritz**

Chuck Ingraham **Gary Engle**

BOTTLING COMPANIES

Bottling companies of Sonoma County, like all other areas and territories across the United States thrived on the sales of mineral water and flavored sodas. Glass factories had molds of various sizes and shapes. An experienced workman (Glassblower) could produce approximately 80 to 100 soda bottles per day.

Those companies wishing to have their bottles cast in special molds could have their company name, trademark, address and/or other information embossed (cast) on the bottle.

Bottles with trademarks such as eagles, pelicans, bears and other animals are especially desirable to collectors.

A number of different companies in Sonoma County area purchased bottles in different styles, shapes and colors. Examples of the glassblowers craft still exist, often with an indication of the company name.

HOW GLASS IS MADE

Glass is formed by the fusion of sand and alkali, generally soda or potash. When the mixture is heated it can be molded into any shape desired.

The materials used in manufacturing common glass came from various areas: sand from Oakland and Monterey, lime from San Jose and soda ash from England.

Arsenic is used to give glass brilliancy. Black oxide of manganese from Red Rock is used to remove the green color of iron oxide, giving glass an amber tint. Hungarian black lead is also added to give glass an amber tinge. Zaffre produces a blue cobalt color.

Molten glass is allowed to cool, and when it is soft enough to be shaped without cracking, the craftsman (Glassblower) takes a blowpipe which is approximately six feet long, and places the required amount of melted glass on the end of the blowpipe.

He then rolls the mixture on a slab called a "marver" and blows through the pipe until it assumes the desired size and shape.

When formed, the bottles are placed in an oven called a "lear" to begin the "annealing" process. Glass is heated, and then allowed to cool very slowly because any item which cools more slowly inside than outside is liable to break because of the derangement of atoms being crushed by unequal tension. Thick glass is used in bottles that requires extreme heat allowing both sides to cool (anneal) at the same rate of time.

After the bottles are annealed, they are then sorted by holding them up to the light enabling the glassblower to detect any flaws or imperfections. Rejected bottles are sent back to the furnace to be melted and perfect bottles are cased for shipment.

SODA POP

The term "soda pop" was coined with the advent of the soda bottle. In 1873, a man named Hutchinson patented a soda bottle with a glass-rod stopper inside the walls of the bottle.

When the bottle was filled the glass-rod stopper would rise into the neck and because of the carbonation would seal the bottle. The glass-rod would protrude approximately one-half inch out of the bottle.

When a person wanted to open the bottle he/she would hold the bottle in one hand, and form a fist with the other hand and hit the bottle top pushing the stopper back into the bottle.

The glass-rod stopper would re-enter the bottle creating a "pop" from the gas (carbonation) rushing out of the bottle, hence, "soda pop."

SELTZER BOTTLES

Many of you remember the Marx Brothers and the Three Stooges' zany chases with seltzer bottles, always good for a laugh as they invariably sprayed the hostess or a dignified guest at a party.

The primary purpose of a seltzer bottle was not comedy but fresh carbonated water for alcoholic beverages.

Many seltzer bottles were made in Czechoslovakia and shipped to the United States. Seltzer bottles were made of unusually thick glass to withstand the pressure of the carbonation.

Seltzer bottles with local labels include bottles from Santa Rosa, Petaluma, Healdsburg, Sebastopol and Sonoma.

BOTTLE ARCHAEOLOGY

Finding old bottles is an art in itself. Bottles surface regularly at flea markets, garage sales, grandma's attic and at times in the walls of old buildings that are being renovated or demolished.

Bottle collectors known as "diggers" have access to old land plot maps that show where houses were located. If you live in an older home, don't be surprised if someone knocks on your door and asks if he/she can probe your backyard.

All towns had outhouses (privies) before the advent of modern sewer systems. When an outhouse outlived its usefulness, it was filled in the same as any land dump. Bottles and other debris were thrown into the hole in order to fill it up.

This became a perfect sanctuary for bottles. The dirt and debris composted around the bottle creating a soft grave for the glass. A digger will see a low spot in a yard and use a metal probe approximately six feet long to poke into the ground as a feeler.

The probe will have a ½ inch cup on the end of the tip. When the probe is pushed into the ground, one listens for the sound of glass while trying to locate a hot spot for bottles and other artifacts.

When the probe is pulled out of the ground the digger checks the cup on the tip of the probe to identify the soil and other foreign particles brought out of the ground.
After a location is chosen the digger will normally dig approximately 5 to 6 feet into the former privy. The dirt is clean as it has composted through the years, allowing the digger soft access to the treasure.

Treasures are not always found, of course, and many a digger has come away with worthless common bottles. Most difficult is when a unique or rare valuable bottle is discovered and it is cracked, broken or only pieces found.

BUILDING A COLLECTION

AMASSING A COLLECTION:
Being a serious collector of pre- Prohibition bartender/cocktail books, old flat top and cone top beer cans, Sonoma County beer and soda bottles, advertising, trade tokens, memorabilia, etc.; I walk through antique stores, flea markets, yard and estate sales, at a fast pace scanning for items related to my collections.

After my first pass at these events I then reverse my travels and now take more time in looking at items with more care. If it's an event with interesting items I may walk each row of tables several times.

Yes, I try to be among the first at any show or sale as the competition is definitely in line when the door or gates open. I do have an array of "pickers" who will find items for my collection (at an inflated price) which is appreciated.

EBAY:
Ebay has certainly changed the field of collecting both good and bad. The good side it has brought us a chance at items that we never had seen or heard of before. The bad news is that the price for an item on Ebay can be inflated plus the cost of shipping.

Another problem of Ebay is that pickers will now purchase anything at flea markets and garage sales that they used to pass on with the intent of placing it on Ebay hoping to make a profit.

It's also not uncommon that a home owner having a garage or estate sale has looked on Ebay at similar items and seen an inflated "buy it now" price and think that their item is worth as much or more no matter the condition or missing parts.

CLUBS AND ORGANIZATIONS:
Being a member of specific groups and organizations helps you network your collection and interests. Being a member of Beer Can Collectors of America (BCCA), 49er Chapter of the BCCA in Watsonville, North Bay Antique Bottle Collectors in Santa Rosa, and San Francisco Postcard Collectors, United States Bartender's Guild (USBG), American Museum of the Cocktail, has helped establish me and my collections to others with similar interest.

I'm also a member of the Sonoma County Historical Society, Petaluma Museum, Windsor Historical Society and the California Historical Society in San Francisco.

I also give history lectures and put on displays at the Santa Rosa Library Historical Anne and Windsor Historical Society. Friend and fellow collector Merle Avila currently has a great Sebastopol display at the Sebastopol Historical Society.

At these events one would be surprised who you will meet and who has a few items of interest or is related to a brewer, soda manufacturer or sales person of the past.

Buy! If your first impression is that it's an item that will fit into your collection purchase it immediately. If you set it down chances are it won't be there when you return. Yes, it may be a duplicate but don't be disappointed as you can sell or trade it to another collector. If possible, carry a detailed list of items in your collection as it's easy to purchase duplicates as your collection expands.

CONDITION:
We all want the choicest mint item. Sorry but it doesn't always happen that way. With extremely rare items and if I don't have that particular item I'll purchase the item in most any condition with the intent of upgrading in the future. It may be a week or several years later but a replacement comes with time. Normally with time and inflation you can then sell the item that you replaced for more than you paid for it.

BOTTLES:
Examine bottles carefully; run your fingers around the lip and base of the bottle feeling for chips, nicks or "flea bites." Hold the bottle towards light or the sun looking for hairline cracks and other imperfections.

A rare bottle that is in perfect condition may be worth several hundred dollars but any and all imperfections reduces the value considerably. Bottles that have been dug can be cleaned by a professional like Lou Lambert for a nominal fee.

BEER CANS:
I personally don't like rust; however, there are those that don't care about the condition of beer cans, all they want is an example. On-line there is a group known as the "Rusty Bunch" who dig and collect dented and rusty beer cans. I have to admit they keep the hobby interesting and come up with variations and previously unknown examples.
Rare beer cans command top dollar and have increased in value every year that I can remember. A key can in 1990 that was over-priced at $12.00 can now be worth several hundred dollars.

GO-WITHS:
Among other items that are collectable are go-withs; advertising, foam scrapers, ashtrays, bottle caps, porcelain stoppers, tap handles, old match book covers, church keys, ice picks, etched glassware, coasters paper labels, neon's etc.; with brewery names on them. These items can be a challenging collection in their own right.

COCKTAIL/BARTENDER GUIDES:
When collecting and purchasing rare books, especially pre- Prohibition, look for missing pages, pencil marks, notations and especially mold. Mold will spread through a collection in a heartbeat.

Should you purchase a rare book for your collection and discover that it has mold between the pages place a sheet of Bounty paper towels in the book between each page and it will absorb the mold. However, keep this book in a plastic bag away from the rest of your collection.

Weevils and mites are also a concern with old books and I have found that by placing the book in a plastic sleeve after adding just a "flash" spray of Raid in the bag eliminates the bug problem.

FORCED COLLECTIBLES:
Stay away from "forced" collectibles like Beanie Babies, Cabbage Patch Dolls, and most anything you see advertised on TV. There is millions of each item made and geared towards Grandma during the holidays to give to children.

PERSONAL CHOICE OF COLLECTIBLES:
My personal choice of collectibles is San Francisco, small town California, Nevada, Wells Fargo, northern California especially Sonoma County. I certainly won't pass on choice advertising, rare bottles and beer cans, and Sonoma County items.

I always keep reference books in my SUV to assist with estimated prices and rarity. Be aware that some collectible reference books the estimated prices are inflated and many reference books are not written by collectors but authors paid to "research" items to be included in the book.

VALUES:
The value of any and items is between what the sell wants and the buyer will pay. At times I've passed on an item that was priced at $20.00 because I was willing to pay $15.00 only to see the same item valued at $75.00 six months later.

If you collect local bottles, for instance Santa Rosa, you'll find that a local name item in Santa Rosa at $20.00 and the same bottle located in Modesto for $10.00. The question is; do you need the bottle and want to pay the price.

In my situation I buy the bottle at $20.00 and then find a duplicate two weeks later at $10.00 or if I pass on the $20.00 bottle I never see another one for three years. So I buy it when I see it as I can always trade off one. Truthfully collectibles are a better investment than the 2% interest you get at the bank or the risk of the stock market. Knowledge is power.

NEW FINDS:
You may have purchased a "one-of-a-kind" item years ago valued at $300 however, at a garage sale there were two or more cases of the item in mint condition that have been stored for years. Now your $300 item is worth $20.00, well, at times that are the chance and risk of being a collector.

REPRODUCTIONS/FAKES:
Be aware of rare items showing up on the market in vast numbers all of a sudden. If it has a value, it can and will be reproduced. Examples are canning jars, Wells Fargo belt buckles (which they never made) brothel tokens, old tin toys, etc.

TOUCHED UP ITEMS:
Some items like advertising no problem, it may affect the value but unacceptable for many items including tins.

OTHER COLLECTORS:
Never be embarrassed to ask other collectors about any article you have doubts about be it rarity, condition or pricing. You'll be amazed the help and advise you will receive. No one can know everything.

DEALERS:
Truthfully it's "Buyer Beware." More dealers than not have a clue of all items in their shop. They purchased an item, did little if any research, and now it's in the display case with a price tag. They may have looked on-line (Ebay) and saw a similar item and that's the price their now asking.

Advantage or disadvantage? It depends; I've seen where a dealer matched an expensive rare mint item price-wise with an off-grade item at the same low price and where a dealer has matched an off-grade common item price-wise with a rare mint item.
Buyer Beware!

BOYES SPRINGS HOT SPRINGS

Sonoma Index-Tribune – February 10, 1906
Opening of Bottling Works at Boyes Hot Springs Sunday

The new bottling works at Boyes Hot Springs here at the already famed Boyes' mineral water is put up for the market, was formally opened on Sunday with appropriate ceremonies in the presence of a large number of friends of the enterprising proprietor of the concern, John W. Kelly.

Capt. H. E. Boyes, from whom the mineral springs take their name, made an appropriate speech and his remarks called forth a hearty applause. The machine was then set in motion, and the water carbonized and Mrs. Boyes had the distinction of bottling the first bottle of the mineral water. The water was sampled by all present and much success prophesied for it.

The ceremonies concluded with an elaborate dinner, which Messrs. Kelly, Schlessinger, and Lichenberg were the principle speakers, enlivening the company with wit and repartee, whose sparkling quality was only exceeded by the mineral water itself.

Sonoma Index-Tribune – February 10, 1906

The opening of the bottling works and putting on the market of Boyes' mineral water is a fine time for Sonoma Valley, as it is real industry of the kind we need more of. We need new industries and men like Mr. Kelly who will push them along.

Sonoma Index-Tribune – August 3, 1907
Agua Caliente Water for the Market

Theodor Richards expects to have his bottling works operation within a short time and the waters of Agua Caliente Springs will then be put on the market on a large scale.

The capacity of the bottling establishment will equal anything of the kind on the coast where natural mineral beverage is put up. The water is a soft sulphur water and is bottled in three sizes and attractively labeled. It will do much to advertise the virtues of the Springs and Sonoma Valley as a summer and health resort.

Sonoma Index-Tribune – April 28, 1908

We rise to remark that Sonoma Valley was entitled to mention in the recent editorial of the Chronicle wherein California mineral springs were extolled and many less famous of our own spoken of.

The gist of the article was to the effect that Admiral Evans' presence and improvement at a California spring will be a world-wide advertisement for our resorts and that the demand for the bottled products of our liquid panacea in increase accordingly. We our glad of these predictions and do believe that the merits of California mineral water is being realized with great rapidity.

We are fortunate to possess in Sonoma valley springs such splendid properties and now that the waters are being bottled and shipped out and it is not necessary for Mahomet to come to the mountain, we are going to get a reputation for this splendid natural product of our sulphur springs.

It is being brought about through the enterprise of Mr. John Kelly of Boyes' water fame and Mr. Theodor Richards of the celebrated waters of Agua Caliente Springs, both of whom should not be underestimated for the work they are doing in revealing Sonoma is peer in mineral waters by putting the article so energetically on the market.

Sonoma Index-Tribune – June 27, 1908

J. W. Kelly has placed the agency of Boyes' Hot Springs Mineral Water with Goetze, Spiro and Goetze proprietors of the Majestic Bottling Company of San Francisco.

****** The following excerpt from **CALIFORNIA HUTCHINSON TYPE SODA BOTTLES** by Peck & Audie Markota.

Charles Reiners and John C. Breig established the Eureka Soda Works in 1872 at 541 and 543 Bryant Street, relocating to 723 Turk Street in 1874.

Breig left the company in 1880 and partnered with George Schafer and started Pacific Soda Works. Reiners operated the company until 1884 and sold to Louis Haake and August Hagerdorn.

Louis Haake and August moved from Turk Street to 233 Hayes Street in 1890, then to 1756 Ellis Street in 1895. In 1898, they incorporated and changed the name to Eureka-California Soda Works.

After the 1906 earthquake destroyed both the Eureka California and Popular Soda works, John W. and Edward H. Goetze owners of the Eureka California Soda Water Company and Isaac Spiro owner of Popular Soda Water Company formed the majestic Bottling Company in 1907 at 20 Biedman Street near Ellis in San Francisco.

The bottled ginger ale as well as soda water in a Hutchinson bottle until approximately 1909/10. The Hutch bottle must have had a paper label as the embossing was on the bottom of the bottle. The embossment stated *"MAJESTIC BOTTLING CO. S. F."*

I believe the reason that the bottles were embossed on the bottom of the bottle was because hutch bottles were placed in the case upside down to keep pressure on the seal of the bottle and it would be easy to identify their bottle because the bottles were inverted.

It is estimated that approximately 1910 they expanded to other flavors; orange grape, lemon, strawberry as well as ginger ale and soda water in crown top bottles.

Sonoma Index – Tribune – May 22, 1920
JACK KELLY SELLS BOYES
MINERAL WATER COMPANY

Jack Kelly who for the past fifteen years has been owner of the Boyes Springs Mineral Water Company has sold out his entire interest to San Francisco parties. The deal was consummated last Monday and by it the new owners come into possession of the bottling works at Boyes Springs and right to bottle the famous water which is now well known all over the Pacific Coast.

Mr. Kelly did some splendid boosting for Boyes Water and the Sonoma Valley during the many years he handled the product of our famous springs. He will continue to reside at Boyes with his family in the attractive bungalow which they own there. Jack will represent several beverages including the popular "Orange Crush." The purchasers of Boyes water rights are headed by a woman, Mrs. Peterson, who controls the new company.

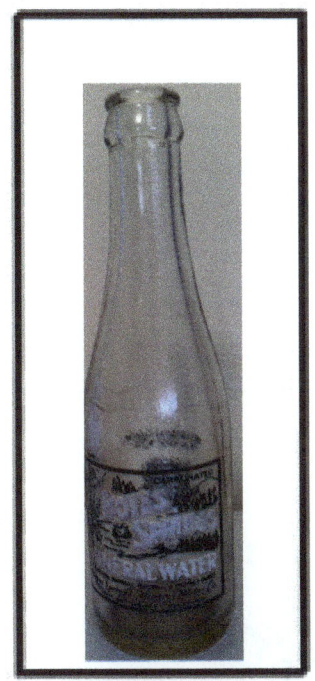

K - 1

K - 83

F. O. BRANDT - HEALDSBURG, CAL.
By Frank Sternad and revised by John C. Burton
Published in the Glassblower – May 1970

The pine and redwood boxes were branded "F. O. B." packed with bottles of sparkling beverage and shipped by wagon to all corners of Sonoma County in the Gay 90's. To popular resorts such as The Geysers and Skaggs Hot Springs, to Pop McCray's at Preston Bridge and the U. S. Hotel in Cloverdale, and to saloons everywhere such as the one at Trenton in the Olivet district near Santa Rosa. To all of these the F. O. B. brand was familiar. It denoted the brewery of Frederick Otto Brandt in Healdsburg and the bottles contained a fine local brand of beer. By 1895 F. O. Brandt was operating in full swing.

Steam Beer was a specialty and this delicate product had to be delivered in small barrels to its destination the same day as brewed, refrigeration being what it was in those days. Brandt's three sons, August, Frederick and William each had become actively engaged in the prospering business to help it grow.

Having a large family, Brandt eventually decided to undertake the bottling of beer from other breweries in addition to what he produced himself. The bulk beer arrived in Healdsburg by rail in large oak barrels and his amber bottles began to carry the labels of such companies as the Buffalo Brewery of Sacramento, National Brewery of San Francisco, and Enterprise of San Francisco and became a major distributor north of Healdsburg of Grace Brothers Santa Rosa.

Frederick Otto Brandt had known beer all his life. Born in Germany and migrating to Green Bay, Wisconsin as a young man, he finally came west to Healdsburg, California in the 1880's. He moved his family into a large Victorian style home on University Street between Matheson and North Streets and erected his brewery on the same property.

Photo from Healdsburg & Northern Sonoma County;

Quart   **Quart**   **Crown Top Quart**   **Pint**

Crown Top Pint   **Half Pint**   **Half Pint**   **Stopper**

Hutch
B on bottom

Hutch
Blank bottom

Hutch
No CAL on face

Crown Top

Non-Footed

Footed

HEALDSBURG

Shining On: the White Star Saloon, Healdsburg
By Merle Avila

The White Star Saloon was located at 101 West Street, corner of West and Matheson (now Healdsburg Ave. and Matheson) in Healdsburg, California. Gum & Jeffry formed a partnership July 24, 1902. Joe Jeffrey was arrested for selling liquor to minors. Following are a couple of the contemporaneous newspaper accounts of the facts of the case, along with a selection of tokens from the establishment identified by their "K" numbers (for Charles Kappen, author of the reference book, California Tokens).

Healdsburg Tribune, April 2, 1909

On Saturday last Marshal Ben Barnes took into custody five boys who were in a state of intoxication. The boys were locked up. They had been discovered near the Railroad track at the end of West Street. They had in their possession a jug of wine and all of them but one was in a beastly state of intoxication. Monday Deputy Sheriff Barnes took the boys to Santa Rosa and turned them over to the Juvenile department of the Superior Court Tuesday morning. Mr. Joe Jeffry was arrested by Sheriff Barnes on the charge of selling liquor to minors. He was taken before Justice Raymond and fined $100.

Whether or not this will end the matter we are not informed but this we do know, that such fragrant violations of the laws of the State and the municipality, deserve a more drastic treatment than a money fine. The Board of Trustees has it in their power to suspend or revoke licenses in such cases. Every saloon keeper in town believes in law and order ought to join in a petition to the Board to revoke the license.

Healdsburg Tribune, April 16, 1909

The city dads met in special session on Monday night to consider the complaint against the Gum & Jeffry saloon for selling liquor to minors. In anticipation of a "fine old time", the hall was packed to suffocation. It was a mixed crowed.

The banker, the business man, the saloon keeper, and the preacher, the prohibitionist and the common boozer gave each other the elbow touch, craned their necks and swayed back and forth to get comfortable standing room. After a few preliminaries which nobody cared for outside the board and which took the place of the friendly boxing that always preceded the main event, time was called and the contestants entered the ring.

The public farce, for farce it was, from start to finish, was well acted. Some of the stage settings were interesting. The first picture of interest was a silver haired barrister whom the people have honored to seat in the halls of the Congress, a man whose personal knowledge of the evils of the dram shop among the youth of the land would make an interesting chapter in juvenile history, appeared for the defense of a confessed violator of the law and uses his brilliant wit to block the wheels of justice, to throw obstacles in the way of full investigation of all the facts. Another picture worthy of study, brought out in the testimony, is of a father going into the accused saloon and buying beer at the bar for himself and his boy. The father it seems to me is a greater criminal than the saloon keeper and is evidently guilty of the offense of giving liquor to minors. The license that ought to be revoked is the license of such a man to bring children into the world to debauch their lives and damn their souls.

From the testimony it is exceedingly doubtful if justly in the reform school. Jeffrey and night watchman Harris each swore they didn't know Darrell from Jack. It may be that the State is "whipping the wrong boy." We suggest that in order to be certain they had better send Jack there also and to make sure throw in the old man. Character witnesses to prove the good character and reputation of the accused were admitted, but evidence to show the general reputation and the character of the place was shut out. The testimony of the boy himself taken by the District Attorney of the County was excluded on the technicality. The fact so stated that the boy had been getting liquor all around town was not disputed by any of the saloon men present.

The contention of Judge Barham and the decision of the board to limit the investigation to the specific charge of selling liquor to Darrell Duncan is contrary to Justice and contrary to law, as set forth by Judge Lawlor and Dunne in the graft cases and also Judge Seawell in the Rowland case. The whole thing was a mix up from the beginning to end in effort to palliate the alleged offense. We were gratified to hear Mr. Jeffrey and Gum both swear that they have no "side entrance to their saloon and no gambling tables or chairs in the rear of their bar. Two witnesses swore that they had seen minors in the saloon but it seems the boys went in there to eat tamales.

"The tamales at the White Star Saloon are the best", we don't like the tamales at the other places. The meeting was long drawn out.

Near the midnight hour, Ralph Thompson made the opening address to the board. It contained some most excellent truths that the saloon men may well consider. Judge Barham made a short talk in a perfunctory way showing that he felt that his speech was unnecessary. After the Thompson speech the Chairman got into a little scrap with the teachers. The Chairman thought the preachers most too exclusive in their efforts against the saloons, that they want to take them all out and are not willing that the bibulous inclined shall have even one place in which to quench their throat for alcoholic stimulants. It looked like for a little while that the ministers were going to be put on trial for their temerity and disorderly conduct in preferring charges against a saloon keeper.

Rev. Shearer however came to their rescue and succeeded in pouring oil on the troubled waters, so that the ministers got away without having their licenses to preach the Gospel in the city of Healdsburg revoked.

Finally the board went into executive session and after consultation, reached the conclusion that the evidence was not sufficient to justify surface the revocation of the license of said Gum & Jeffrey, but the chairman was requested to give Mr. Jeffry and the balance of the saloon keepers in town a curtain lecture urging them to take warning from result of the present investigation and keep the minors who got drunk out of the sight of Ben Barnes for Ben will nab them sure, and the men that sell them the booze, and if they are brought before Judge Raymond, he is silly enough to believe that laws placed on the statute books ought to be enforced even against saloon keepers.

Whatever may be said of the others, Mr. Barnes and Judge Raymond have done their duty as sworn officers of the law. They have paid no attention to legal quibbles and technicalities. Special thanks to Holly Hoods, Healdsburg museum curator, for helping me with researching the White Star Saloon; Jack Trotter, Healdsburg historian; and to The Healdsburg Tribune newspaper.

White Star Trade Mirrors

K-4 K-5

K-41

K-42

K – 43

K-44

K – 45

K-63   Unlisted variety of K-63

SQUEEDUNKS
Darrell Duncan is Squeedunks performing in front of the White Star Saloon. Squeedunks, also known as Calithumpians, were organized groups of men who would dress up and perform political satire for the public from the 1860s to the 1930s. Squeedunks came to festivals to scare people and participate in an annual parade through downtown Healdsburg every 4th of July starting in 1908. Some squeedunks were scary and others funny. Rumor has it, when children would misbehave, their parents would tell them, "You better watch out or the squeedunks will come and get you!"

LYTTON SPRINGS

In 1900 William H. Bone managed the Peoples Mineral-Hygiene Company (P. M. H. Co.) The C. H. B. on the bottom face of the bottle is thought to be a misprint which was meant to represent William H. Bone. In 1902 Duncan Springs Water Company merged with Peoples Mineral Hygiene Company becoming the California Mineral Company.

(Face)
LITTONS
MINERAL
WATER

(Reverse)
Vertical Print
HEALDSBURG

Richard and Bev Siri bottle

OCCIDENTAL BOTTLING WORKS

One year only, 1908, owned by Bert Philbrick.

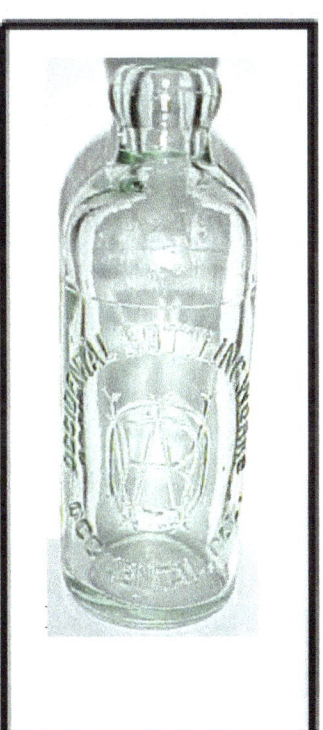

Not much information about Bert Philbrick. His family was farmers in Occidental. He was born October 25, 1881, married June 13, 1907 and died in June 19, 1947.
Records show he was a laborer, operated Occidental Soda Works, and then worked for Hudson at Santa Rosa Soda Works, becoming a mechanic for Associated Oil.

He lived in Bodega while operating the Occidental Soda Works so I imagine most of his distribution was along the coast.

- 1900---805 Healdsburg Ave., Santa Rosa---Laborer
- 1910----No address/private St., Bodega,---Soda Maker
- 1920---315 S. Davis St.---Mechanic, Associated Oil

City Directories
- 1903---730 Tupper St.---Employee, W. H. Hudson
- 1905---732 Charles St.---Teamster, W.H. Hudson
- 1908---Occidental---Soda Manufacturer
- 1909---Occidental---Soda Manufacturer
- 1911---315 S. Davis St.---Bottler, W.H. Hudson
- 1913---315 S. Davis St.---Bottler, SR Bottling Works
- 1915---315 S. Davis St.---Bottler, SR Bottling Works
- 1918---315 S. Davis St.---Machinist, Associated Oil

PETALUMA - HEALDSBURG

THE HISTORY OF B. F. CONNOLLY & BROS.

BY FRED LEONI

Bernard Francis Connolly was born in Keady, Northern Ireland in 1836. Sometime in the middle or late 1850's, young, red-haired and adventurous Bernard, along with his older brother Michael, heeded the call of California's gold fields and set off to make their fortunes. The brothers sailed to the Isthmus of Panama where they disembarked and proceeded across the Isthmus by foot. After arriving in Panama City and finding no ship available to San Francisco, they purchased two mules and commenced to make their way north by land.

They first went to Nevada City. The brothers must not have had much luck as they eventually made their way to Sonoma County settling near Healdsburg. Here on July 1, 1861, they leased from W. H. Litton, the Geyser Soda Springs located four miles north of Healdsburg for (as stated in the lease) "the sole use and purpose of bottling and selling the water and no other." They leased the springs for five years for the sum of $600.00.... "To be paid in good merchandise redwood rails and posts at the rate of eight dollars per hundred."

Michael remained in Healdsburg and Bernard went to San Francisco to be the agent for Geyser Soda Water. On November 30, 1865, the brothers again leased the springs for a five year period, this time for $1,000.00. Connolly and Bro. remained in San Francisco until 1868 or so when he moved to Petaluma. The location of their soda works in Petaluma is not known, but it is known that on June 28, 1871, Connolly & Bro. purchased a lot in the general area where the State Theater is today. Here they erected an iron-front, fire proof building for their business.

On October 12, 1872, B. F. Connolly married Miss Minnie Bayliss, daughter of Captain Thomas Fulsher Bayliss, one of the earliest pioneers of Petaluma. They would later rear eight sons and one daughter.

On August 27, 1875, B. F. Connolly bought a lot on the corner of 6th and B Streets and then moved his soda works to this location. It is around this time that Michael left the business, later becoming a deputy sheriff in Santa Rosa where he died on November 22, 1887 at the age of fifty-four.

Bottles of soda and sarsaparilla; and 700 dozen champagne cider; which are distributed in Sonoma and Marin counties; amount of sales $10,000.00."

Connolly remained in business until the late 1880's or early 1890 are when he sold his business to John Endres. At this time the soda works was supposedly the Capitol Soda & Bottling Works. Research is yet to be made to link this name with Capitol Bottling Works. On December 29, 1898, B. F. Connolly died from a stroke brought on from his getting into an argument and letting his Irish temper get the best of him.
Fred, thank you for the article....................JB

Face   **Reverse**   **Face**   **Reverse**

Face   **Reverse**   **Face-Reverse Blank**

PETALUMA

ENDRES & CO.

In 1895 John Endres purchased Connolly's bottling plant and operated it until 1903 when he sold to Louis Schmidt. John F. McCarthy was Endres's manager. The location of the facility was 6th and B Streets (725 B Street)

Reverse – **THIS BOTTLE REGISTERED**

PETALUMA

CAPITOL BOTTLING WORKS
BY ED MANNION

Photo courtesy of Petaluma Library

"Like a stage setting, area residents watched a spectacular fire that destroyed a building at Stanley and Upham Streets last night" said the Petaluma Argus-Courier on March 16th. The story went on to say that the building was empty and its use unknown. Bottle hunters could have told the reporter that the wooden structure was a portion of the Capitol Bottling Works, a Petaluma enterprise memorialized by glassware in the collections of several North Bay relic buffs. There was a lot of glassware on the property but unfortunately it was all in small pieces, numerous smashed bottles having been under the flooring in a basement of sorts. No digging has been done on the site as far as is known.

An exact history of the capitol name seems hard to come by and members of the Northwestern Bottle Collectors Association are urged to keep eyes open for information in the course of allied research. For instance, the writer went to the Sonoma County Clerk's Office expecting to find the bottling company listed in a ledger either under incorporation certificates or fictitious names. Nothing found. So-to the regional directories.

Scudder's rare Petaluma City Directory of 1895 lists a Capital Soda and Bottling Works, 725 B Street, I. F. McCarthy, Manager. No bottles are known for sure from that address. A neat, yellow house stands there today and the owner expressed amazement that her little bit of God's green earth had such a commercial background. The same address is given in the Oppenheimer County Directory of 1899-1900.

A copy of the 1903-04 Directory of Santa Rosa City and Sonoma County lists the Capitol Bottling Works at Washington Street, corner of Keokuk.

In 1905, the Kingsbury's Directory first mentioned the company at the corner of Stanley and Upham. L. G. Schmidt was the proprietor. The LS monogram is on bottles in collections today. A special edition of the Petaluma Argus in June 1907 mentioned the firm in part as follows: "The business was established over twelve years ago but has been under the present ownership for the past year. The premises occupied comprise a large and modern plant, equipped with every modern appliance for successfully carrying on business, including ample cold storage facilities. The firm manufactures all kinds of soda waters and are bottlers of the celebrated Wunder Lager and Steam Beer. They are also agents for Jackson's Napa Soda, Quiro's Seltzer, and various kinds of mineral waters. They bottle two carloads of beer a month; selling large quantities of their goods to local trade.....Able proprietors are H. Hammerman and J. Jarr."

The HJ monogram is another identification known to regional bottle collectors. Hammerman is sometimes seen with two "n's". The Argus statement, "established over twelve years ago" would place Capitol natal date before 1895. Unfortunately, the Petaluma newspaper files, almost solid from 1855, are broken through the 90's.

The story becomes confused because a Petaluma lithograph by W. W. Elliot usually dated 1885 though finished in 1884, shows no brewery on B Street but does depict an unnamed brewery at the corner of Upham Street. Stanley Street isn't shown but something that looks like "Happis" is pictured instead. Perhaps this should have read "Harris" which today is only a block long southeast of Upham and cutoff by private property.

The map date of the litho is 1884 or 1885 which is ten years before the Argus-Courier story mentioned the Capitol Bottling Works as being on the Upham-Stanley site. Maybe the newspaper had the wrong information or maybe there was another brewery on the site before Capitol took over.

The eight county directory of 1885-86 published by L. M. McKenney, lists the Sonoma Brewery of Petaluma, with George Griess as proprietor. No address is given. In 1875, the Sonoma Brewery was at nearby Baker Street near Western, now a vacant lot. Michele and Griess started that enterprise two and one-half years before. George Griess is remembered today as owner of the United States Brewery once located on the southeast corners of Bodega and Upham Streets. Amazing that at least three breweries were located in such an adjacent area.

Only eleven Capitol bottles were listed in the Frank Sternad-George Epperson publication of the Northwest Bottle Collectors Association. Eight of these are in the writer's (Ed Mannion's) collection........

Ed, thanks for your research, you will always be remembered......................JB

CAPITOL BOTTLING WORKS
Louis Schmidt - 1903 - 1907

Quart Large LS

Pint Large LS

Pint Small LS

Half Pint Small LS

LS on bottom

Bottom blank

CAPITOL BOTTLING WORKS
H. Hammerman & Johannes Jarr
1907 –1915

Torliatt Family Photo - Thank you Lee

Capitol

Misspelled Capital

Pint

PETALUMA SODA AND BOTTLING WORKS
George Bruchner & Henry Zeh
1895 - 1905
631 Main Street
Eugene E. Klammer & Eugene E. Malz
1905/1907
Klammer & Malz also had a bottling plant in San Rafael
PETALUMA SODA & SELTZER WORKS
(Business name and address change)
Corner Upham & Stanley Streets
Eugene E. Klammer
1907
Northeast corner Washington & Hooper Streets
1102 Washington Street.
Charles (Henry) Hammerlind & Aleck Larson
1907-1915
215 G Street
Southeast Corner 3rd & G Streets

Klammer & Malz purchased the **Petaluma Soda & Bottling Works** in 1905 changing the name to **Petaluma Soda & Seltzer Works.** The address listed for them is the Southeast corner of Upham & Stanley Streets. They bottled soda, sarsaparilla, and seltzer and distributed Cascade Beer.

In 1907 Malz left the partnership, and Klammer moved the **Petaluma Soda & Seltzer Works** to the northeast corner of Washington & Hooper Streets. The address is listed as 1102 Washington Street and phone number as Red 481. Klammer & Malz also had a bottling plant in San Rafael.

Later in 1907 the Petaluma Soda & Seltzer Works was sold to Charles Hammerlind and Alex Larson who operated the facility until 1915. The address changed to the southeast corner of Third & G Streets (215 G Street). They added Coca Cola to their line of products and the company now became known as Petaluma Soda & Seltzer Works aka Coca Cola Bottling of Petaluma & Sonoma.

Larson operated the plant as sole proprietor from 1915 until 1924. He sold to S. R. Kristiansen in 1924. Kristiansen added a special Petaluma drink named "Chickaluma" described as a delicious soda water somewhat of a grenadine punch.

The Petaluma Soda and Seltzer firm has had three locations. Each new proprietor relocated the firm. Klammer and Malz had a bottling plant in San Rafael and purchased the Petaluma Soda and Seltzer firm in 1905. They started bottling soda, sarsaparilla, seltzer and distributing Cascade Beer. Each proprietor continued bottling with Kristiansen adding a special Petaluma drink named "Chickaluma" described as a delicious soda water somewhat of a grenadine punch.

In 1930 the plant was purchased by Coca-Cola Bottling Company. In 1948 new equipment was installed increasing bottling capacity to 120 bottles per minute. They also started bottling Mission Orange, Delaware Punch, Calso Water, Cliquot Club, Ginger Ale and other flavors. They also became local distributors for Falstaff and Lucky Lager beers, and Italian Swiss Colony wine and Petri wine.

Dan Brown Bottle

Footed Non-Footed

 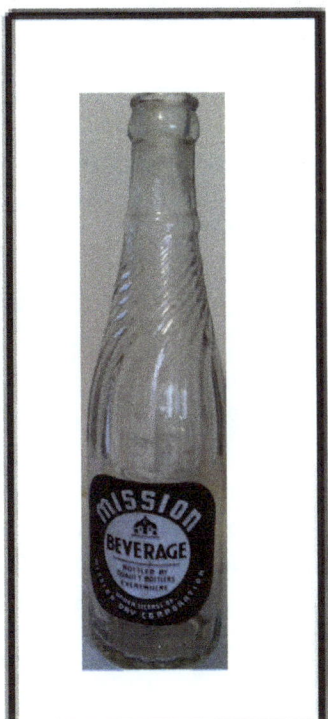 

E. Klammer
Ebay

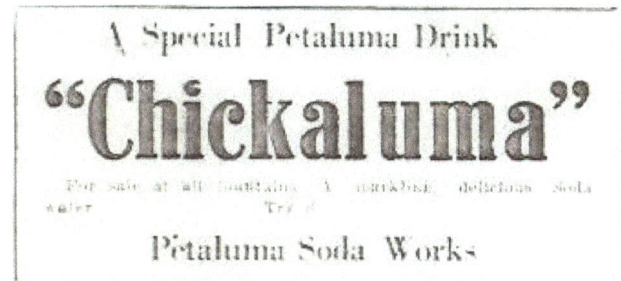

PETALUMA

PETALUMA BREWERY
631 North Main Street
Main Street near Bridge Street
Now known as Lakeville

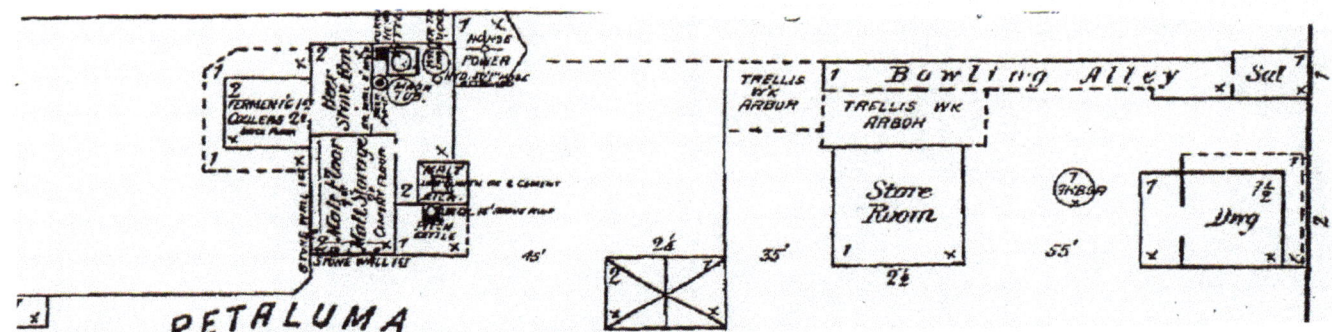

Consisting of the following buildings:

- Power House
- Malt & Flour Dry Storage
- Beer Storage Room
- Furnace for Kettle and Pitch Kettle
- Main Brewery
- Fermenting Cellar
- Separate storage for Wood

===

PETALUMA BREWERY

- Frederick Christlich & Erbe
- 1855/ March 1864
- 631 North Main Street (Main Street near Bridge Street)

===

PETALUMA BREWERY

- Frederick Christlich & Thielmann
- March 1864/1867
- 631 North Main Street

ALE AND BEER!
PETALUMA BREWERY.
At the North End of Main Street

Messrs. Christlich & Thielmann , of the Petaluma Brewery, are constantly manufacturing large quantities of Ale and Lager Beer, which they are prepared to deliver promptly in any part of Petaluma or Sonoma County. All orders from families faithfully attended to, either for Quart Bottles, Five or Ten Gallon Kegs.

===

PETALUMA BREWERY

- Frederick Christlich
- 1867 - 1870
- 631 North Main Street

F. CHRISTSLICH, Would respectfully inform his friends and the public in general, that he has enlarged his brewery, and is now prepared to fill all orders, in quantities to suit, for his

PREMIUM LAGER BEER & ALE

He has also fitted up a place of resort in fine style at his Brewery, where the public are invited to call and see for themselves. He has also established a Depot for the sale of his justly celebrated Lager and Ale, on Main Street, next door below the central Mill, at G. William's Saloon, where all orders will be promptly attended to, and where kegs, bottles etc., may be left. Try and give me a call.

F. CHRISTSLICH   (Notice misspelling of Christlich)

==

PETALUMA BREWERY

- Charles Efinger & Co.
- 1870 - 1872
- 631 North Main Street

Petaluma Brewery!
North End of Main Street

CHR. EFINGER & CO., Proprietors, Having purchased the above well-known Brewery and Grounds, the subscribers desire to invite the attention of all in want A NO. 1 ARTICLE OF LAGER BEER, to their establishment. Being practical Brewers and of many tears experience, they can and will furnish their customers with AS GOOD AN ARTICLE OF BEER in all respects, as can be produced by ANY BREWERY IN THE STATE. A trial is respectively asked. Beer delivered to hotels, bars, or families in town or forwarded to any part of this or adjoining counties.

CHR. EFINGER & CO.

Petaluma, Jan. 20th 1870.

==

PETALUMA BREWERY

- C. Blatz & H. Schierhold
- 1872 - 1876
- North Main Street

C. BLATZ & H. SCHIERHOLD, PROPS.

THE ABOVE NAMED BREWERY MANUFACTURERS the best and most beer of any Brewery north of San Francisco. Beer delivered to any part of the city free of charge.

- Schierhold was a cigar manufacturer in Petaluma in 1874.
- Approximately in 1876 his partnership with Blatz dissolved and he began a partnership with Wohler doing business at the Relief Saloon on Main Street also in Petaluma. Schierhold and Wohler were also the sole agents for Felsen Bottled Beer in Sonoma County. Quart bottles sold for $1.50 a dozen.
- In 1895 he was proprietor of the Capitol Saloon in Santa Rosa located at 822 Main Street.

PETALUMA BREWERY

- George Robuson
- 1876/1884
- 631 North Main Street

===
PETALUMA BREWERY FACILITY

- George Fischer
- 1884
- 631 North Main Street

George Fischer opened a winery in the old brewery building.

===

PETALUMA BREWERY

- Caroline Robuson (Widow)
- 1885 – 1887
- 631 North Main Street

===
PETALUMA BREWERY

- Jurgen Henry Gerckens (Leased from Mrs. Robuson)
- 1887 - 1889
- 631 North Main Street

- Brewery burns completely down August 16,1889
- Jürgen is also proprietor of Union Hotel 3rd & B Streets.

===

PETALUMA BREWERY
(Mellitzer Builds New Brewery on Location)

- P.Mellitzer
- 1893 - 1917
- 631 North Main Street

===
PETALUMA BREWERY

- Joseph T. & Frank P. Grace
- June, 1917 – April 15, 1918
- No production
- Probably purchased to obtain rights to grain allotment because of WWI.
- May have salvaged brewery equipment for Santa Rosa.

PETALUMA

EAGLE BREWING COMPANY

- **Thomas G. Edwards**
- **1856 – 1872**
- **One Mile North on Santa Rosa Road**

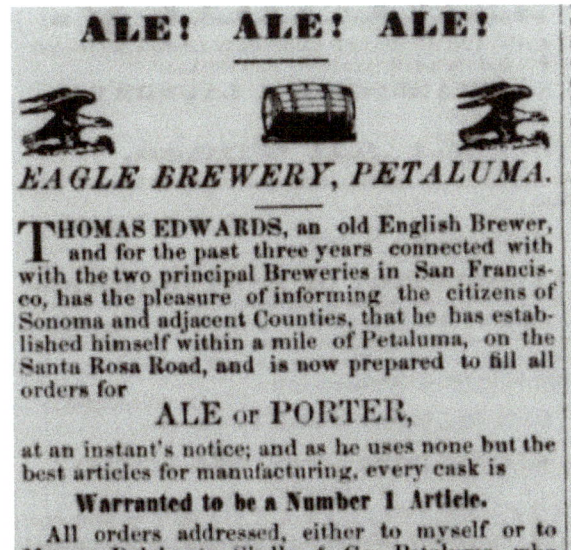

ALE! ALE! ALE!

EAGLE BREWERY, PETALUMA.

THOMAS EDWARDS, an old English Brewer, and for the past three years connected with the two principal Breweries in San Francisco, has the pleasure of informing the citizens of Sonoma and adjacent Counties, that he has established himself within a mile of Petaluma, on the Santa Rosa Road, and is now prepared to fill all orders for

ALE or PORTER,

at an instant's notice; and as he uses none but the best articles for manufacturing, every cask is

Warranted to be a Number 1 Article.

All orders addressed, either to myself or to Messrs. Delahenty, Skelly & Co., Petaluma, who are my authorized Agents, will meet with a prompt and faithful reply.

A fair trial of my article is respectfully and confidently solicited. Call and try it. o22-tf

Partnership Notice.

DELAHANTY & BROWN having formed a co-partnership to transact the wholesale Wine and Liquor business, at Kent & Smith's old stand, Main street, Petaluma, will keep constantly on hand, at San Francisco prices, the choicest assortment of Wines and Liquors, Ale and Porter, ever offered in Sonoma county. Also Soda Water and Sassaparilla Manufacturers, and Sole Agents for Edwards' Eagle Brewery, Petaluma.

Petaluma, March 18, 1858–4w.

PETALUMA

SONOMA BREWERY OF PETALUMA
MITCHELL BREWERY
PETALUMA UNITED STATES BREWERY

- Edward Franz
- 1867 – 1875
- Corner Bodega & Upham Streets

- Charles & Fred Mitchell
- George Greiss
- 1875 – 1899
- Corner Bodega & Upham Streets

- George Greiss
- 1901– 1916
- Corner Bodega & Upham Streets

New Advertisements.

SHERIFF'S SALE.

ANTON MEYER VS. CHARLES MITCHELL, George Griess and August Wickersheimer. Order of sale and decree of foreclosure and sale.
Under and by virtue of an order of sale and decree of foreclosure and sale issued out of the Superior Court of the county of Sonoma, State of California, on the 24th day of November, 1886, in the above entitled action, wherein Anton Meyer, the above named plaintiff, obtained a judgment and decree of foreclosure and sale against Charles Mitchell et al., defendants, on the 24th day of November, 1886, for the sum of $3,364.77 in United States gold coin, besides interest, costs and counsel fees, I am commanded to sell all those certain lots, pieces or parcels of land situate, lying and being in the city of Petaluma, county of Sonoma, State of California, and bounded and described as follows: Designated and numbered on the official map of said city of Petaluma as lots number two hundred and eighty-two (282) and two hundred and eighty-three (283).
Public notice is hereby given that on TUESDAY, the 28th day of December, 1886, at 12 o'clock M. of said day, in front of the Court House door (Fourth street entrance) of the County of Sonoma, I will in obedience to said order of sale and decree of foreclosure and sale, sell the above described real estate, or so much thereof as may be necessary to satisfy said judgment with interest, costs and attorneys fees to the highest and best bidder for gold coin of the United States.
T. C. BISHOP, Sheriff.
December 1, 1886.   de4 w4t

PETALUMA

UNITED STATES BREWERY

- **George Griess proprietor**
- **511 Upham Street**

PRESTON CALIFORNIA – NORTH OF CLOVERDALE
BARCAL BEVERAGES
John Kolling Proprietor

Mineral Water **Mineral Water** **Cream Soda**

Root Beer

Strawberry

Cloudy Orange

Orange Soda

Cloudy Lemon Soda

Lemon Soda

SANTA ROSA

IXL SODA WORKS
Tupper Street between "E" Street & Petaluma Avenue
E. J. Stollar & R. H. Stollar - 1889 - 1891

Not much (if any) research has been done regarding the Stollar Brothers.

**Information and photograph found and summited by John Louder
Edward John Stollar 1849-1927
1888 Voter Registration listed as living in Santa Rosa -"soda maker."**

Press Democrat August 1889

E. J. Stollar & Bros. presented this office Wednesday with a case of their delicious sodas and sarsaparillas. The pleasant flavorings of vanilla, lemon and other well-known extracts make a pleasant drink. The firm is located on Tupper street.

SANTA ROSA

GILT EDGE BOTTLING WORKS
500 "B" Street (Corner of 5th & B Streets)
George Szameitat - 1899 - 1900

George Szameitat owned the Gilt Edge Saloon at 507 "B" Street next door to his bottling works from 1899 until 1900. His bottling of soda water only lasted one year. .

Not only are his bottles extremely rare but they were not annealed, (reheated a second time) and all know bottles have cracks or stress fractures throughout the bottles. The Gilt Edge Hutchinson bottle is aqua with a tooled top. Highly desirable, this rare bottle is seldom seen in collections.

Gilt Edge sold March 14, 1900 to **Jacob Joost,** formerly of the Court House Exchange. He has purchased the Gilt Edge saloon on Fourth Street, and has already taken possession. The Gilt Edge has always been recognized as one of the most successful resorts of its kind in this city and under its new management the place will undoubtedly retain all its old-time popularity as well as gain many new ones. **George Szameitat,** the retiring proprietor, after spending a few weeks at Skaggs' springs will start on an extended visit to Germany.

Yesterday, November 1, 1905, the Gilt Edge saloon business, conducted by the late **Jacob Joost,** on Fourth Street, was sold to **Brown & Gnesa** of the Oberon, who take possession today. Yesterday bids for the business were opened in the law office of Colonel L. W. Juilliard, attorney for the Joost estate, and the sale to **Brown & Gnesa** was ratified by the administration.

SANTA ROSA

ROSE CITY SODA WORKS

John J. Mathews & James L. Roberts - 9 & 11 Main Street - 1905 - 1911
James L. Roberts - 9 & 11 Main Street - 1911 – May 14, 1918
Henry A. Cross – May 14, 1918 – March 24, 1919
Ross Garrison - March 24, 1919 – April 2, 1919
Albert Visser – April 9, 1919 – July 21, 1919
Elmer Brown & Son - 215 D Street – July 21, 1919 - 1939

John J. Mathews and James L. Roberts started the **Rose City Soda Work's** at 9–11 Main Street in 1905; it lasted until 1911 when Mathews sold is interest. Mathews purchased half-interest in the Grapevine Saloon at 531 – 4th Street.

Mathews and Roberts bottled ginger ale, cream soda, Sarsaparilla and various other flavors in returnable crown top bottles. These bottles were embossed and are found in clear, aqua, and purple. They also bottled Seltzer at this time.

After Mathews sold his share, Roberts continued using the name "**Rose City Bottling Company**" and relocated to 215 D Street.

Thanks to Jim Famini who purchased a 1918/1919 Sonoma County Recorders book I was able to track the interesting history of the sales of Rose City Bottling Works.

On May 14, 1918, James L. Roberts sold for $10.00 in gold coin, the entire business to Henry A. Cross the entire business including; carbonating machine, bottling machine, siphon machine, three phase electric motor, Bishop-Babcock carbonate pump, bottle washing machine, filtering machine, all siphon cases, all soda cases, all oyster shipping cases, all soda water bottles, all siphon bottles, all oyster bottles, all carbonic acid gas, about 12 dozen quart bottles, about 70 dozen split bottles, beef cubes, celco, labels, scales, measures, demi-johns, jugs, all machinery, barrels, tubs, pans, and all furniture and fixtures.

On March 24, 1919, Henry A. Cross sold the entire package listed above to Ross J. Garrison for $10.00 in gold coin. On April 2, 1919 just nine days later, Garrison sold the entire package as listed for $10.00 in gold coin to Albert Visser. Visser continued the business at 215 D Street until July 21, 1919 when he sold to Elmer E. Brown & Son (Claude C. Brown). Brown continued bottling various flavors until 1939 when he sold to Mike Capitani's father.

SANTA ROSA

Burton Postcard

                                                              M & R   **JLR**

Started in 1905, Rose City Soda Works bottled various sodas including the usual sarsaparilla, ginger ale, cream soda, and other flavors. They also bottled seltzer water. All of their soda bottles are crown top never having used Hutchinson style bottles.

Mathews left Rose City Soda Works in 1911 and became partners with Walter Jones at the J & M Saloon (formerly the Grapevine Saloon). The saloon closed in 1918 because of prohibition.

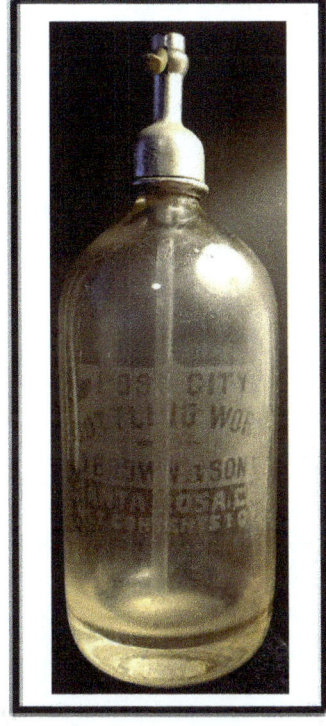

Louder Bottle

ROSE CITY SODA WORKS
E. BROWN & SON BOTTLING WORKS

ROSE CITY SODA WORKS

BROWN & SON

Only Sterilized Plant
In Sonoma County

Our Motto: Cleanliness,
Carefulness and Quality

SOLE BOTTLERS FOR

Hires, Cherry Blossom and Orange Crush Sodas—Bartlett, Celso and Napa Soda Mineral Waters.

215 D Street   Phone 1189   Santa Rosa, Cal.

SANTA ROSA

T & H BOTTLING

The 1876 issue of the *Santa Rosa Democrat* lists the T&H Bottling Company, on the east side of Metzger's Santa Rosa Brewery at 112 Second Street. John Thomas and a Mr. Haskins were partners from 1876 until 1878 when Thomas became the principal owner and the name was changed to T & Company.

Both the T&H and T & Company bottles have gravitating stoppers. The phrase "soda pop" comes from these types of bottles, because the glass stopper with a rubber grommet was inside the bottle and forced up by carbonation and sealed the bottle from the inside out. This type of bottle is known as a gravitating stopper with an applied top. After the bottle itself was blown, stopper inserted, a top was applied and then the bottle was annealed (heated a second time) sealing the bottle.

Both these bottles, T& H and T & Co. have "Sonoma Cal." embossed on their face referring to to Sonoma County, not to the city of Santa Rosa. The bottles were patented by John Matthews on October 11, 1864 and have been found in both aqua and lime green. Both types of bottle are extremely rare and command premium prices to collectors.

In 1882, T & Company was sold to **George Ford and Conrad Johnson**, who were together until 1885, when Johnson sold his interest to William T. Ashley. Ford and Johnson's bottles were "Hutchinson" bottles, a new style replacing Matthews gravitating stopper. Ford and Johnson's bottles are plain on the sides, suggesting a paper label, and are embossed on the bottom of the bottle which was unique in our area. Ford & Johnson bottles are not as desirable to collectors because of the plain sides and embossing on the bottom of the bottle, however, they do fill in a piece of history.

SANTA ROSA

SANTA ROSA SODA WORKS
Patrick J. Sullivan
160 Third Street - 1875 - 1883

The Santa Rosa Soda Works was owned by Patrick J. Sullivan from 1875 until 1883 and located at 160 Third Street. Sullivan's bottles are gravitating stoppers, similar to Thomas and Haskin's who also produced soda waters.

Like **T & H and T & CO**. bottles, Sullivan's first bottle has **P. J. S. & CO. - SONOMA CAL.** on the face which refers to Sonoma County, not Sonoma, California. This bottle was used until 1883 and the new design stated **P. J. SULLIVAN - SANTA ROSA, CAL**.

This kind of bottle was known as gravitating stopper with an applied top. After the bottle was blown, the stopper was inserted, a top applied and then (reheated) annealed, sealing the bottle. These bottles were patented by John Matthews on October 11, 1864.

When Sullivan closed his business and left the name Santa Rosa Soda Work's unprotected, Hudson & Palmer picked up the business name and used it as well as their Santa Rosa Bottling Work's name.

SANTA ROSA

CHRONOLOGICAL ORDER OF SANTA ROSA BOTTLING WORKS

November 27, 1875

> SODA MANUFACTORY.—P. J. Sullivan has established a Soda Manufactory on Third street, between A and B, and is ready to supply the trade in that line at lowest market rates. Mr. Sullivan has had many years experience in the manufacture of Soda Water, and feels fully competent to satisfy the demands of the public. Orders sent by mail or express will receive prompt attention. Address P. J. Sullivan, Santa Rosa Soda Works, Santa Rosa, Cal. no27w1t

April 3, 1886

Santa Rosa Soda Works.

> V. L. Pieratt has purchased the Santa Rosa Soda Works, and will commence manufacturing immediately. Mr. Pieratt has many friends who will be pleased to see him make a success in his new business.

Press Democrat, Number 232, 3 April 1886

> V. L. Pieratt's Santa Rosa Soda Works are running in full blast. The delivery wagon will henceforth make its daily trips.

Somewhere n this time frame George Ross is a partner with Valentine L. Pierrat.

Press Democrat, Number 202, 8 March 1889

> George Ross has sold his interest in the Santa Rosa Soda Works to W. W. Skaggs. The firm name will be Hudson & Skaggs.

Ross has sold his share to W. W. Skaggs.

1889
Hudson and father-in-law James S. Palmer purchase an interest in
Santa Rosa Bottling Works in partnership with W. W. Skaggs.
Company becomes known as Hudson & Skaggs.

SANTA ROSA

1889

William H. Hudson & James S. Palmer purchase W. W. Skaggs interest in Santa Rosa Bottling Works.

1893

Deed from March 2, 1893 shows Hudson bought a piece of property from Linn Bledsoe. The property is on "The Old Road from Santa Rosa to Sebastopol" and along side the SF&NP railroad. (3rd & Roberts Avenue)

1901
Father-In-Law James S. Palmer died October 10th

Press Democrat, Number 15, 19 January 1909

W. H. Hudson, proprietor of the Hudson Bottling Works, Santa Rosa, has leased that establishment to John L. Gist and Fred (or LeRoy Emmet Jones) Jones.

Lease Aerated Water Business

The Santa Rosa Bottling Works, conducted for years by W. H. Hudson, has been leased by John L. Gist and Fred Jones, who will run it in the future. Soda waters and oyster cocktails are the specialties of the business and the new proprietors will seek to maintain a good business on the merits of the goods they produce.

Press Democrat, Number 232, 16 November 1909

Dissolution Notice

The undersigned have this day dissolved partnership by mutual consent and the business known as the Santa Rosa Bottling Works will be carried on in the future by L. E. Jones. Dated Nov. 15th, 1909.

11a22   L. E. Jones,
         John L. Gist.

SANTA ROSA

Press Democrat, Number 245, 14 October 1911

> CERTIFICATE OF INDIVIDUAL FICTITIOUS NAME—State of California, County of Sonoma, ss:
>
> I hereby certify that I am transacting business in the State of California, at Santa Rosa, under a designation and name not showing the names of the persons interested as partners with me in such business, to-wit:
>
> Santa Rosa Bottling Works.
>
> Name: W. H. Hudson. Place of residence, Santa Rosa.
>
> State of California, County of Sonoma.—ss.
>
> On the 23rd day of September, in the year one thousand nine hundred and eleven, before me personally appeared W. H. Hudson, known to me to be the person whose name is subscribed to the foregoing instrument and he acknowledged to me that he executed the same.
>
> Witness our hand this 23rd day of September, 1911.
>
> (Seal)   C. O. DUNBAR,
> Notary Public in and for the County of Sonoma, State of California.

April 24, 1924
William H. Hudson sells Santa Rosa Soda Works to Robert "Albert" Callori

1949/1950
Callori starts negations in 1949 with Frank & Hazel Carrey completing sale of Santa Rosa Soda Works on May 25, 1950. They operated the bottling company until 1953/54.

In 1956 the Carrey's purchased the Boyes Springs Mineral Water Company from George Chicazola and operated it until 1972. Chicazola had purchased Boyes Springs Mineral Water in 1940. Prior to ownership of the bottling company he was a truck driver for a brewery.

SANTA ROSA

HUDSON & PALMER
Santa Rosa

Santa Rosa Soda Works, Hudson & Palmer, Proprietors.

Burton Photo

In 1887 Hudson returned to northern California and purchased the Santa Rosa plant from Ford and Johnson, changing the name to Hudson & Palmer, Santa Rosa Bottling Company and continued to operate the facility on 2nd Street. At this time their Hutchinson style bottles were embossed **HUDSON & PALMER – SANTA ROSA BOTTLING CO. – SANTA ROSA**. Within a short time the facility was moved to the corner of 3rd and Roberts Avenue. **November** Hudson's Father-In-Law, James S. Palmer died October 11, 1901 and soon after Hudson changed the company name to Santa Rosa Bottling Works.

Hutchinson style soda bottles embossed SANTA ROSA BOTTLING CO. is more common than their rare predecessor bottles stating HUDSON & PALMER.

Crown top soda bottles started becoming popular around 1905 and Hudson followed the trend. One unusual bottle just located in 2014 is a bottle in transition that has a crown top and embossed with the face of previous Hutchinson style bottles. There are now two known. Hudson progressed to a paper label on his soda bottles. Bottles were recycled and relabeled on his "modern" bottling line that filled approximately 15 bottles a minute. In addition to the

Orange Soda shown here, he also bottled Cream Soda, Strawberry Soda, Lemon Soda, Ginger Ale, Sarsaparilla, Orcherade, and Hires Root Beer.

Santa Rosa Bottling Work's bottling plant.

Santa Rosa Bottling Work's bottling line.

Wm. H. Palmer and delivery truck

Santa Rosa Bottling Work's Sample Room & storage

Quart

Siri Qt. Bottle

Siri Qt. Bottle

Quart

Pint

Half Pint

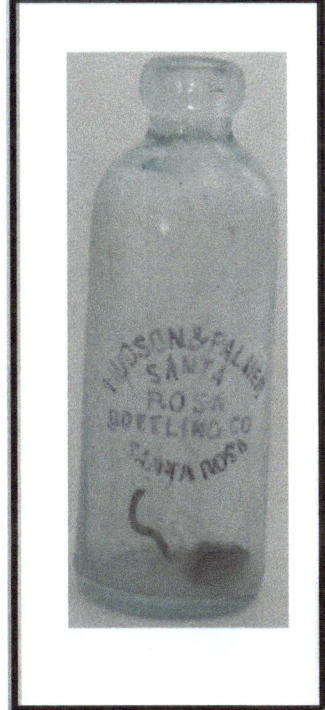   

Transition Bottle

                                                                                                                    Fifth   **Quart**

SHRIMP & CRAB COCKTAILS

In the 1920's and 1930's both oyster cocktails and shrimp cocktails were extremely popular. I would assume that both these cocktails were bottled until either the fad faded or the health department looked at the facility and made them stop bottling these cocktails. Dealing with fresh seafood is much different than soda water. Crab Cocktail. Many of these cocktails found their way into "Speakeasy's" during prohibition.

Albert Callori Bottles

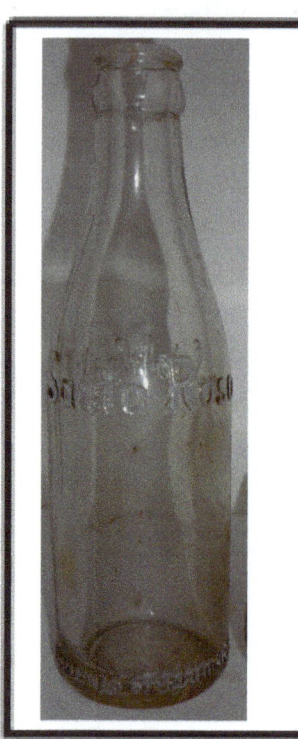

HUDSON PURCHASES CIGAR SHOP
SANTA ROSA
February 1901

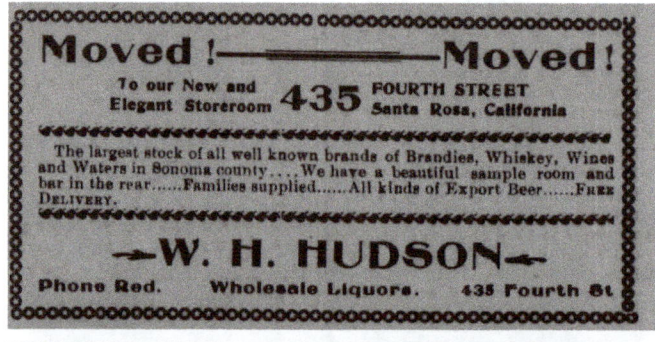

Press Democrat, Number 76, 11 January 1902

JAMES L. HAYWARD
Successor to W. H. Hudson.

WHOLESALE

Liquors and Cigars

AGENT FOR

Cook's Mineral Table Water, Witter Springs Medicinal Water and Pabst Milwaukee Lager Beer

Free Delivery. Phone Red 501 — 435 FOURTH STREET, Santa Rosa, California

CIGAR SHOP BANKRUPTCY

Press Democrat, Number 15, 2 November 1902

Bankrupt Sale

On Wednesday, the 5th day of November, 1902, at 11 o'clock a. m., at the store, No. 435 Fourth street, the stock of goods, consisting of wines, liquors, ale, beer, cigars, barrels, etc., will be sold.

Also one spring wagon, and one set of single harness. Sale will be made at public auction for cash. Store will be open daily for inspection of goods.

11c5   W. H. Hudson, Trustee.

HUDSON PURCHASES
FIRST & LAST CHANCE SALOON
CORNER FIRST & MAIN, SANTA ROSA

Press Democrat, Number 312, 23 December 1903

The above saloon on Main and First streets has been completely remodeled and renovated by the present owners, Messrs. Smith & Borzone, and presents a very attractive appearance. The formal opening will take place on the evening of Dec. 24th and the proprietors extend a cordial invitation to the public to attend. The best of goods kept.   1t

Press Democrat, Number 140, June 15, 1904

H. J. Barzone has sold out his business in the First and Last Chance saloon on Main street to W. H. Hudson. The negotiations were closed yesterday. Mr. Barzone will remain here for a few days at the saloon.

Press Democrat, Number 72, 1 March 1905

Janile and N. Giles Yeager of Geyserville have purchased the "First and Last Chance" saloon at First and Main streets.

**1909 Hudson & McKee Purchase Old Corner Saloon
20 Main Street**

Press Democrat, Number 295, 18 December 1912

COUNCIL REFUSE THREE LICENSES

Action Taken at the Meeting Held Here Last Night by the City Fathers

The three applications denied renewal were as follows:

Ferrari and Moranda, 113 Fourth street; Hudson & McKee, 20 Main street; Lugi Franchetti, Wilson and Seventh street.

SANTA ROSA

GRACE BROS.
1897 – 1966

GB Bottling Line

Grace Bros. Tasting Room Glasses

Grace Bros. "Button" Advertising

Crown Top Beer Bottles

Available in Quarts Also

GRACE BROS. SANTA ROSA BEER BOTTLE LABELS
NOT INCLUDING VARIATIONS

  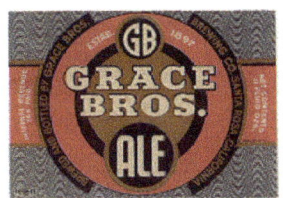 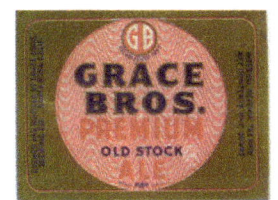
  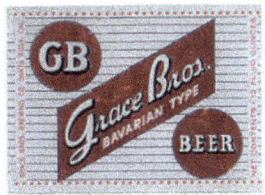 
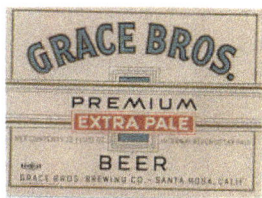   
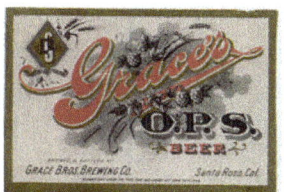   

GRACE BROS. BEER CANS

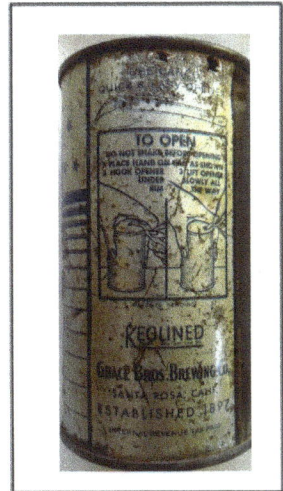

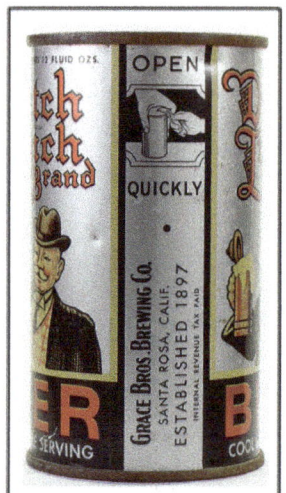

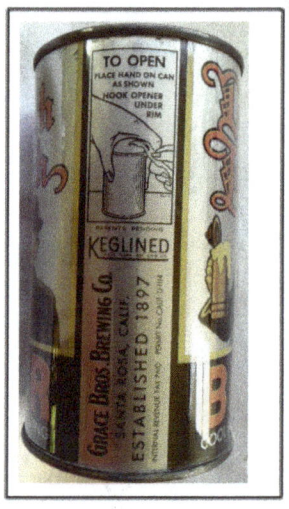

                      Great Beer   Good Beer

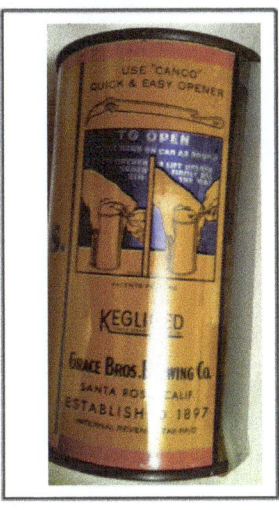

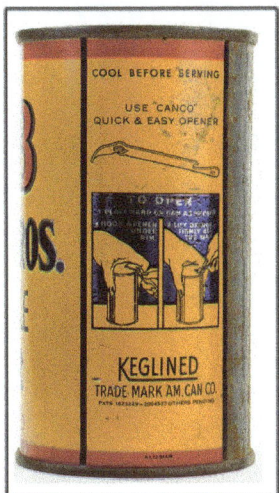

Bock on lid

Red side panel

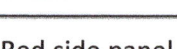

Dark Blue   **Photo**   **Keglined**   **National**

Mayfair Markets   **Quart**

SANTA ROSA

JAMES BRUCKER
Northeast Corners of South A & Petaluma Hi-Way
(820 Santa Rosa Avenue)
1947 - 1955

James Brucker was a distributor of SONOMA CLUB sodas. Ginger ale was his most popular flavor. He also bottled Nehi Beverages and Weilands beer until 1950.

Building was located corner of Santa Rosa Avenue and Bennett Valley Road. Now holding up hi-way 12 overpass.

Brucker's race car having missed the last turn.

SANTA ROSA

ROSELAND SELTZER COMPANY
Samuel Alexander - 611 Santa Rosa Avenue - 1944
300 Chestnut Street - 1947 - 1965

Samuel Alexander bottled sodas and seltzer water. He also was the distributor for Wieland's and Falstaff beers. In 1960 Samuels widow, Rose, also distributed Regal Pale beer.

On July 15, 1947 the business was sold to J. F. Walton of Burlingame, California.

SANTA ROSA
Bud J. Peter
2450 Stoney Point Road
Santa Rosa, Ca
Phone SR 1697-J

BUDOLA – A SPARKLING BEVERAGE

Thinks don't always turnout the way you expect them too. I've spent numerous hours trying to find information regarding Crystal Bottling Works in Sebastopol; probably 60 plus hours at the Sonoma County Annex, the Sebastopol Historical Society and the Sebastopol City Clerk. Zero information, nothing, not even a smell. One reason is that there are so many missing phone books and city directories between the years 1918 to 1938.

As all collectors and historians know is that one thing leads to another. Having had a painted label bottle of Budola in my collection for years it has been assumed by me and others that it was a Callori product when he had his bottling plant on West 7th Street.

In Sebastopol at the Historical Society looking for anything related to Crystal and being tall; I happened upon a 1939 business directory high up on the top shelf in the reference room and while looking through it out comes this ad on the back cover for Budola.

Inside I found the information of a "new to me" bottler in Santa Rosa, Bud J. Peter located at 2450 Stoney Point Road, Santa Rosa. Now my quest has expanded to what years was Peter bottling mixers and was there any other items such as orange, grape, root beer, etc.

SEBASTOPOL

1905/1909
Sebastopol Bottling Works

Ownership: One Hundred percent stock
- E. M. Zimmerman
- R. C. Zimmerman
- A. D. Zimmerman

November 5, 1909
Enterprise Bottling Works
Sebastopol Ice Plant

Ownership: One-Third stock each
- George W. Kingsbury
- Harry B. Morris
- Fred Matthews

September 25, 1913
Enterprise Bottling Works
Sebastopol Ice Plant

Ownership: Fifty percent stock each
- Fred Matthews
- Samuel P. Cleek

March 1917
Enterprise Bottling Works
Name changed to Sebastopol Bottling Works

Ownership: One Hundred percent stock
- F. W. Hardwick

February 1919
Sebastopol Bottling Works

Ownership: One Hundred percent stock
- John O. Button (Botton)

1922
Sebastopol Bottling Works

Ownership: One Hundred percent stock
- George W. Sollars

April 3, 1930
Sebastopol Bottling Works
Coca Cola Bottling Plant

Ownership: One Hundred percent stock
- Edmond Meyer

SEBASTOPOL

Avila Bottle

SEBASTOPOL

 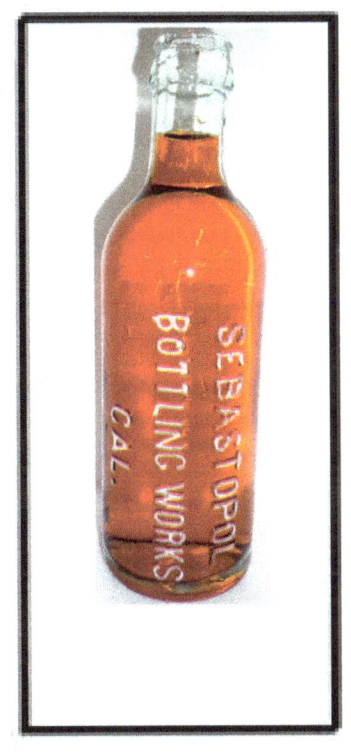 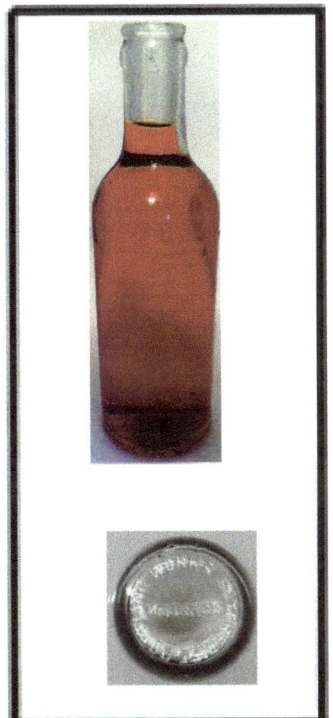 

Crystal Avila Bottle **Avila Bottle** **Avila Bottle**

SEBASTOPOL

Sebastopol Times
November 30, 1923

SOLARS SECURES COCA COLA FRANCHISE FOR BIG TERRITORY

A franchise of considerable importance to Sebastopol and a recognition of the increasing business becoming, done by this community and a local institution has been secured by George Sollars for the White Diamond Soda Works here. This is a bottling franchise for Coca-Cola beverages embracing the territory in Sonoma County north of Cotati.

The local plant is now the largest Bottling Works north of the Bay City and latest addition to the line will still further increase the firm's business. Mr. Sollars secured this franchise and competition with all kindred firms of the North Coast section. A large new truck has been purchased to handle the increased output of the plant.

The Coca-Cola franchise states from the first of the coming year, at which time the name of the local plant will be changed to the Coca-Cola Bottling Works.

Mr. Sollars also handles coal and wood at the local plant. The car has just been received in an ad in this issue calls attention to the fact that a large supply of both coal and wood is now on hand.

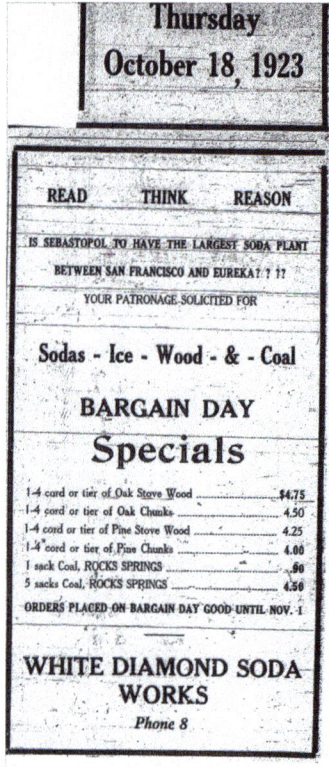

SEBASTOPOL

KIST BOTTLING COMPANY
Mortgage Sept 27, 1949
October 28, 1952 - 1957
Robert Colburn
775 Healdsburg Avenue
Sebastopol, Ca.

SONOMA

SONOMA BREWING COMPANY
Gottlier Kestler 1905/1908
Phillip Scheuer
John Steiner 1908
2nd Street East (North of Spain Street)
Agent for Buffalo Brewing Co.
SONOMA ICE & BREWING COMPANY
John Steiner 1908/1915
Angelo Beretta – Manager - 1913/1929
SONOMA VALLEY ICE & COLD STORAGE CO.
Fred D. Bose 1905/1913

SONOMA

Articles of Incorporation
of
Sonoma Brewing Company
January 12, 1910

Know all Men by these Presents:

That we, the undersigned, have this day associated ourselves together for the purpose of forming a *CORPORATION* under the laws of the State of California,

And we Hereby Certify,

FIRST, That the name of said *Corporation* is

SONOMA BREWING COMPANY

SECOND, That the services for which it is formed are to buy, sell, manufacture, hypothecate, and deal beer, malt, malt products and all brewery materials, supplies and products; to transport and export the same; to acquire, sell, lease, hypothecate, will, construct and operate breweries and brewery plants, stores, warehouses and depots in connection with any of the aforesaid lines business; to acquire, hold, hypothecate, and dispose of all kinds of real and personal property, including licenses, easements, franchises and rights, and to buy, sell and deal in generally all of the products thereof; why, sell, manufacture, hypothecate, lease, and dispose of ice, both artificial and natural, ice products and distilled water, both playing and carbonated, and to acquire, hold and operate, lease ,hypothecate, and dispose of ice manufacturing plants; to acquire, hold, operate, lease, construct, hypothecate, and deal in all perishable foods and generally to engage in and operate a cold storage business; to acquire, hold, operate, lease, construct, hypothecate, and dispose of creamery plants and to buy, sell, hypothecate, and deal in milk and milk products and to engage in the manufacture and disposal of products there from and generally to engage in and carry on a creamery business; to purchase, own, acquire, hold, hypothecate, sell and deal in stocks, bonds as shares of the capital stock and bonds of this and other corporations; and to do, perform and carry out all lawful business, acts and things which the Board of Directors may from time to time deem proper, convenient or necessary for the purpose of expediting and carrying on any of the aforementioned objects and purposes of the Corporation.

THIRD, That the place where its principle business is to be transacted shall be the City of Sonoma, County of Sonoma, State of California.

FOURTH, that the term for which it is to exist is fifty years from and after date of its Incorporation.

John Steiner	600 Shares	$30,000.
H. H. Granice	20 Shares	1,000.
A. Beretta	20 Shares	1,000.
C. Dal Poggetto	10 Shares	500.
H. P. Mathewson	5 Shares	250.

SONOMA

SONOMA VALLEY SODA WORKS
William & Angilina Hurley   1910
J. M. Rogers of Vallejo May 1, 1936
STAR SODA WORKS OF SONOMA
Ernest C. Campbell 1911/1926
L. F. Nieman 1926 -

STAR SODA WORKS
E. C. CAMPBELL, Proprietor
ONLY THE HIGHEST GRADE OF GOODS SOLD
Soda Water of All Flavors
SELTZER WATER
SYRUPS
BOYES WATER
BUY HOME-MANUFACTURED PRODUCTS
Factory Phone 535   Residence Phone 1354

It's fun to be thirsty, for then we little "Thirsties" come on the run to tell you of—

Ward's Orange-CRUSH
for Thirst, also
Lemon-Crush—Lime-Crush

Ward's "Crushes" owe their distinctive and delightful flavors to the natural fruit oils of oranges, lemons and limes. To these have been added pure cane sugar, citrus fruit juices, U. S. certified food color, fruit acid and carbonated water.

STAR SODA WORKS
L. F. Nieman   Sonoma, Cal.

SONOMA

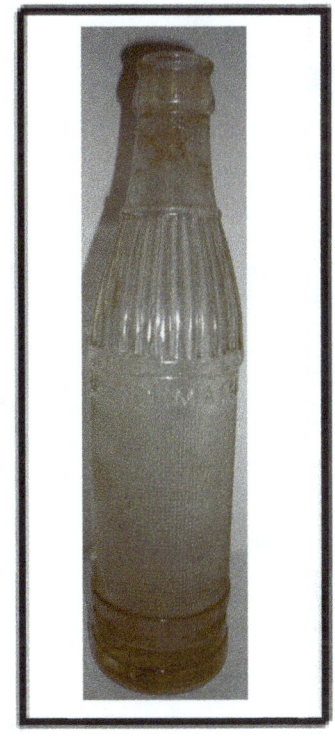

WHISKEY, BRANDY & WINE BOTTLES
FEATURING SALOON & CIGAR TRADE TOKENS

WHISKEY BOTTLES AND SALOON TOKENS

BOULEVARD
John W. Wood
1 Main Street
(Southwest Corner First Street)
1911 – 1913

- John Wesley Wood- March 5, 1868--Dec.19, 1946
- 1909, '10, '11, '13, '15, and '18 directories have him listed as saloon proprietor,
- 1 South Main Street
- Prior to 1909 is listed as blacksmith, 3 Main Street
- In 1913 and earlier, home was at 213 3rd Street
- In '15, it was 706 Hendley
- In '18, it's 727 Santa Rosa Avenue
- 1920 census lists him as proprietor, cigar store (hello, prohibition.)
- 1930, he is in Eureka working as a mechanic
- 1935 and '40, he is in Lake Co. retired
- Buried in Oak Mound Cemetery, Healdsburg, plot- section 2, block 5R

K - 8

CAPITOL SALOON

CAPITAL SALOON
301 4th Street
W. S. Beeker
(March 29, 1889 – 1906)
William A. Ford & John Bayler Proprietors
(1906 – 1913)

Press Democrat, Number 220, March 29, 1889

Opening Night. A cordial invitation is extended to everyone to attend the opening of the Capitol Saloon, Saturday evening March 30, 1889. Mr. W. S. Beeker has spared neither trouble nor expense in fitting up this elegant resort for the comfort of his patrons and will have spread a lunch that the epicures of old, would vie with in paying compliments to.

K – 12 A
Unlisted

K – 12

THE CASTLE

637 – Fourth – Street (Hahman Building)
W. B. Sanborn Proprietor – 1887- 1890
John W. Swank Proprietor -1891 – 1908
Charles Gardner and William Beswick – Proprietors 1909 – 1912
Charles Gardner – Proprietor 1912 -1918

Press Democrat, Number 293, 30 November 1905
J. W. SWANK, Who Successfully Conducts three kinds of business at once.
The old saying that a man can do more than one thing at a time J. W. Swank, who simultaneously is a house mover, contractor and a saloon owner and does three things at once, and does them well. The Castle bar and wholesale store in the Hahman building is one of the best saloons in town.

Press Democrat, Number 167, 18 July 1911
GETTING READY TO BUILD HAHMAN BUILDING
King Crist (Contractor) moved the "Old Castle Saloon" building from the Hahrnan lot on Fifth Street Monday, and a force of men went to work cleaning the lot preparatory to the erection of a modern store building on the lot, extending from Fourth through to Fifth Street. The building has been leased by J. C. Pedersen, who will move his large furniture store there as soon as it is ready for occupancy. It will be built by the Hahrnan estate.

Press Democrat, Number 157, 6 July 1912
Will Improve "The Castle"
Charles Gardner and William Beswick, the proprietors of "The Castle" saloon in the Doyle building at Fourth and 1> streets, are contemplating making a number of fine Improvements in I heir place. They mean to have it one of the most up-to-date and attractive places in the city. They have planned some very neat changes in the place, and when they are finished they will certainly have a pleasing effect.

Press Democrat, Number 145, 19 June 1913
Accepts Position
Will Graham has accepted a position as mixologist at The Castle, Chas. Gardner's saloon on upper Fourth Street. He will be glad to have his friends drop in and see him

Press Democrat, Number 193, 17 August 1915
"CASTLE" SALOON HELD UP BY MASKED HIGHWAYMEN
Sunday Night Robbery
Replete With All Daring of Early Frontier Days
With Modern Crime in the Bigger Cities —
Three Men Robbed
A hold-up was staged in Santa Rosa about half-past eleven o'clock Sunday night which savored of the regular old-fashioned type of frontier days, or things that occur in the bigger cities. There was the tall and the short bandit, the yawning muzzle ends of huge revolvers, the handkerchief-masked laces of desperados. Just the kind of stuff that would make racy reading for the "penny a

THE CASTLE

liner'' for a page or two in a dime novel. The escape and pursuit of the bandits, the attendant thrills given those relieved of their coin, etc., must be included.

Charles Gardner's "Castle Saloon," one door from the corner of Fourth and D streets was the scene. Tim Isles, the barkeeper, Charles Krausse the well-known cigar dealer, and William J. suddenly became aware that the three shadowed bandits came in the swinging doors from Fourth Street burst in and they looked up to see the muzzles of revolvers in the hands of two masked men were covering them. *"Up with your hands, all of you and be quick about it"* one of the fellows hissed.

Tim Isles grabbed a bottle, not sure whether it was a josh or whether the real thing was being pulled off. *"Drop that bottle quick, or I'll shoot,"* muttered the man behind the gun. And did it say to the credit of Isles, he did as he was commanded without further delay. His hands went up- Krausse and Doran very wisely had already submitted. The bandits made the barkeeper open both drawers of the cash register and shell out the content some seventy dollars. *"Open that safe.''* the fellow said threateningly: *"Can't do it, sir; I am only the assistant barkeeper and don't know how."* replied the barkeeper.

"Fair enough, then. Now get back there." The bandits then searched their victims securing about sixty dollars and a watch from Mr. Krausse and $4.75 from Mr. Doran. Isles had no coin other than a quarter in his pants pocket and that was not taken. They Took Drinks. This done, the bandit ordered the barkeeper to put four bottles of beer and a bottle of whisky into a sack that he. carried. This was done. The man then called to his partner, who had remained on guard while the searching of pockets and til had been proceeding, and first one and then the other made his getaway. They hurried up Fifth and crossed to Humboldt Street.

Will Carter, who lives at the Meyer residence, met them and stopped to look at them and the sack they were carrying. *"Get the in there."* shouted one of the men roughly, and Carter stepped inside. At the time Carter was unaware of the hold-up. It did not take the victims of the hold-up long to run outside after the robbers had disappeared and give an alarm. Policeman Shaffer was the first to respond and Policeman Reid and Richardson and Chief Boyes were soon on the scene, together with Sheriff Smith and some of his deputies. All joined in a search of the city and Sheriff Smith took a hasty detour of the outskirts in his automobile.

No clues were obtainable, however, plenty of rumors. Following the hold-up there were many rumors, one of which was to the effect that the men had boarded an automobile on Fifth Street near Mendocino and had made their getaway in that. That theory was soon exploded both by the statement of Carter and by ascertaining the identity of the man whose machine had been noticed and which had aroused suspicion. Thus in brief is told the first story of Santa Rosa's first hold-up in the manner described. Monday night men were on the lookout for any suspicious characters about town. The two bandits wore light overcoats over their suits.

THE CASTLE

Amber cylinder
Tooled top
5th – 11 Inches tall
Rarity: Rare

THE CASTLE
NET CONTENTS
24 FLUID OZS.
SANTA ROSA, CAL.

Unlisted

Unlisted

CLUB SALOON

CLUB SALOON (1908 – 1913)
319 Fourth Street
Edward Allvenn - Proprietor

Sonoma County Library Photo

K – 17

K - 18

Unlisted

COMMERCIAL HEAD QUARTERS

A. B. Stump Proprietor 1886 - 1890
518 Fourth Street
Upstairs

REOPENING!
—OF THE—
Commercial Headquarters!

A. B. STUMP — — PROPRIETOR.

518 FOURTH ST., UP STAIRS.

THIS FIRST-CLASS SALOON WILL BE RE-opened

TUESDAY, MARCH 9, 1886.

The above establishment has been refitted and refurnished, and will always be well stocked with the choicest wines, liquors and cigars. Fine billiard tables and reading room attached.

JAS. S. MENEFEE,

Whose reputation as a compounder of cocktails is so widely and favorably known, will assist Mr. Stump in the management of the establishment.

mar9 dawtf

Commercial Headquarters!

A. B. STUMP — — — PROPRIETOR.

518 FOURTH STREET,

UP STAIRS, NEXT TO DEMOCRAT OFFICE.

THIS FIRST-CLASS SALOON WILL BE RE-opened

Tuesday, March 9, 1886.

The above establishment has been refitted and refurnished, and will always be well stocked with the choicest wines, liquors and cigars. Fine billiard tables and reading room attached.

mar9 dtf

CUB BILLIARD & POOL PARLORS

225 – 4th Street

K – 23

K - 24

K - 119

GERMANIA HOTEL

105 – 107 – 109 Fourth Street
John Haas Proprietor – 1885 – 1887
Walter Schmid & John Ritter Proprietor – 1887 - 1903
Edward Pflugi Proprietor 1903 - 1909
Joseph Weinzerl Proprietor 1909 -

Press Democrat, Number 225, July 9, 1903
Germania Hotel Sold
Walter Schmid has disposed of his business at the **Germania Hotel** on Fourth Street and on Friday he will turn over the business to the new proprietor, a gentleman from San Francisco. Mr. Schmidt's health has not been very robust of late and he will take a prolonged rest and change.

Press Democrat, Number 201, September 8, 1906
TAKES A VACATION Oscar Mathews, Well Known Hotel Manager, Enjoys Rest
A well-earned vacation is being enjoyed by Oscar F. Mathews, the **manager** of the St. Rose **Hotel** since it was opened. Mr. Mathews has severed his connection with the hold, and for a few weeks he will take a rest. Mr. Mathews is widely known in the **hotel** business, and possesses the happy and desirable faculty of pleasing the traveling public. Consequently both at the St. Rose and at the **Grand Hotel** of which he was chief clerk for a long time, he made both places very popular and gained many friends by his courtesy and attention.

Press Democrat, Number 137, June 11, 1907
Charged With Embezzlement
Oscar Johnson, who was formerly clerk at the Germania hotel, was arrested in Vallejo Monday by Constable J. H. Boswell on a charge of embezzlement. He is charged by Proprietor Pflugi of holding out moneys collected while he was clerk and since leaving the hotel and keeping the money.

Press Democrat, Number 220, September 21, 1907
Santa Rosa John **Ritter** and Walter Schmidt THE GERMANIA **SCHMIDT & RITTER** Fine Wines, Liquors and CIGARS AT THE SAME OLD STAND 481 Fourth Street Santa Row

Press Democrat, Number 45, February 26, 1909
The **Germania hotel,** on lower Fourth Street, has a new owner, Edward Pflugi having sold the hostelry to Joseph Weinzerl, a well-known **hotel** man, who formerly conducted establishments In Sacramento, San Francisco and elsewhere. About three weeks ago Mr. Pflugi, whose health has not been good, departed for Hot Springs, Ark., and his wife will leave here in a day or two to join him there. During their residence in this city and their conducting of the **Germania hotel,** Mr. and Mrs. Pflugi have made many friends, and have been very successful. They hope someday to again take up their residence In Santa Rosa. The new **proprietor** is wished a full measure of success also. Bring your magazines and pamphlets to the Press Democrat office and have them rebound in modern style and the right order.

GERMANIA HOTEL

Press Democrat, Number 104, May 6, 1909
Germania Hotel Renovated
Joe Weinzerl, the new proprietor of the Germania Hotel, has just finished having the hotel thoroughly renovated. Everything has been put in first-class shape, and Mr. Weinzerl says that the comfort of his guests will be his first thought. He is an experienced hotel man, and has made many friends since his arrival here.

Press Democrat, Number 158, July 4, 1913
John Haas' Funeral Held
The funeral of the late **John Haas,** former proprietor of the Germania Hotel In this city and who died on his ranch near Melitta, several days ago, took place from the funeral apartments of Lafferty & Smith. The Rev. Father Cassin officiated and the interment was In Calvary cemetery

Unlisted

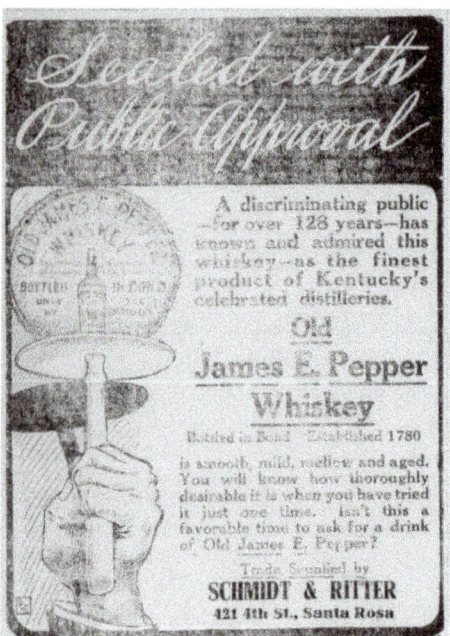

GRAPE VINE SALOON

Sonoma County Library Photo

R. E. L. McReynolds & Austin Leary
1887 – 1890
11 – 13 Mendocino Avenue
Wm. T. Orr & A. B. Stump
1890 – 1905
11 – 13 Mendocino Avenue
Charles Orr
1905 – 1907
11 – 13 Mendocino Avenue
Walter Jones & John O. McIntosh
1907– 1909
Corner 5th & Mendocino
(Same location after quake)
John O. McIntosh - Proprietor
1909– 1911
Corner 5th & Mendocino
GRAPE VINE LIQUOR SALOON
313 Mendocino Avenue
1911 - 1917
Dan Pickin – Proprietor

A. B. Stump had a saloon upstairs at 104 Main Street from 1885 to 1889. In 1890 he and William J. T. Orr formed a partnership and opened the Grape Vine Saloon on Mendocino Avenue. The address is listed as 313 Mendocino Avenue, between Fourth and Fifth Streets in the 1905 city registry.

November 1, 1905, another business change took place yesterday when Charles Orr, purchased the Grape Vine saloon business on Mendocino Street, so long conducted by his brother and the late John A. Stump, of the old firm of Orr & Stump. It is understood that Mr. Orr will have a partner. Like his brother he has a large circle of friends.

In 1907, the business was sold to Walter Jones and John O. McIntosh who were partners for only about 6 months with Jones selling his share and becoming partners with Mathews at the J & M Saloon (Jones & Mathews). McIntosh ran the Grape Vine until 1911 when he sold to Dan Pickin who had been a shoemaker. Pickin continued the business until Prohibition.

The Grape Vine eventually became the Bank Club owned by Primo & Kitty Rocco. Rocco sold to Alf Lepori and Peter Biocioni in 1957.

Please note that there are two bottles, *Orr & Stump*, listed in *Early Bottles of Sonoma County* by Frank Sternad and in *Picnics, Coffins, and Shoo-Flies* by John Thomas. Thomas's mentions Doc Ritz as his source. I have never seen these two bottles, nor has anyone else that I've talked to, and have been unable to verify their existence. I will mention them here in this publication on speculation.

GRAPE VINE

Size:	Half Pint
Style:	Coffin
Year:	1900
Height:	6 Inches
Type Top:	Tooled
Color:	Clear
Bottom:	1560
Rarity:	Rare

**GRAPE VINE
MENDOCINO
AVENUE
SANTA ROSA, CAL.**

GRAPE VINE

Size: Half Pint
Style: Coffin
Year: 1900
Height: 6 Inches
Type Top: Tooled
Color: Clear
Bottom: 1560
Rarity: Rare

**GRAPE VINE
MENDOCINO
AVENUE
6 FLUID OZ.**

GRAPE VINE

Size: Half Pint
Style: Coffin
Year: 1900
Height: 6¼ Inches
Type Top: Tooled
Color: Clear
Bottom: 1560
Rarity: Rare

**GRAPE VINE
MENDOCINO
AVENUE
SANTA ROSA, CAL.
NET CONTENTS
6 FLUID OZ.**

GRAPE VINE

Size: Pint
Style: Coffin
Year: 1900
Height: 7¼ Inches
Type Top: Tooled
Color: Clear
Bottom: 1308
Rarity: Rare

**GRAPE VINE
MENDOCINO
AVENUE
SANTA ROSA, CAL.**

K- 40

K - 41

K - 42

GRAND HOTEL

Main Street
Phillip Morshead – Proprietor – 1883 – 1889

GRAND HOTEL BAR & BILLIARD PARLOR
Corner Third & Main Street
Frank Kelley - Proprietor
Morris Wise - Bar Keeper

GRAND HOTEL – FASHION STABLE
Phillip Morshead
William H. Underhill

GRAND EXCHANGE (Inside Grand Hotel)
Corners Third & Main Streets
Phillip Morshead - Proprietor 1886
George Morshead - Bar Keeper
J. F. Gonzalez - Bar Keeper

GRAND EXCHANGE SALOON
H. Mutz Proprietor – Proprietor 1887
George Morshead - Bar Keeper
J. F. Gonzalez - Bar Keeper
Peter Dolan - Bar Keeper
Phillip Morshead - Bar Keeper

GRAND HOTEL BAR ROOM
George Morshead in white coat
SONOMA COUNTY LIBRARY PHOTO

GRAND HOTEL

Shining on: the Grand Hotel, Santa Rosa
by Merle Avila

By the 1870's Santa Rosa was a regional center frequented by tradesmen and merchants who stayed in downtown hotels. The Grand Hotel, built in 1873 and shown here at Main and Third Streets, had 40 rooms and 13 suites. As stagecoaches, trains, and wagons carried travelers through the far reaches of the north coast, hotels and resorts sprang up to serve their needs. One of the most prominent of these was the three-story Grand Hotel. It had running water, gas, marble washstands, carpeted halls, and black walnut and rosewood furniture.

The Grand had many merchants and professionals in residence. In 1889 a physician, a city councilman, and the editor of the newspaper, The Republican, all made their homes at the Grand Hotel. The bar at the Grand was the town's social center by the turn of the century. Stanley, Jeblett, and Julliard sold stoves, hardware, and agricultural implements from the same building. Competition was keen among the hotels as each instituted omnibus service from the two railway depots to their respective establishments. One evening in the fall of 1896 The Grand Hotel had a big night. It was recorded that L. Genazzi, driver for the Occidental Hotel, fell asleep at the Southern Pacific Depot and George Oakes, the Grand's driver, "took all the arrivals that night" to the Grand.

The Grand Hotel was destroyed in the 1906 earthquake. One of the few people on the street in the early morning hours when the earthquake struck saw the Grand Hotel collapse following a sound like wagon wheels on a cobblestone drive and a visible wave passing through the street. Landlord Michael McDonough and his grand piano were shaken out of the building and onto the sidewalk. Mr. McDonough was last seen sitting safely on top of his piano covered only by an American flag.

K - 33

GRAND HOTEL

The Grand Hotel in 1885. By the end of the 1800's Santa Rosa had about 100 buildings and 400 citizens. The Grand before the 1906 quake, looking south from the top of the Courthouse along "Main Street" now Santa Rosa Avenue.

Grand Hotel after the collapse during the 1906 quake.

HOTEL LA ROSE

Corners 4th & A Streets
A. E. Chartrand – Proprietor (1905)

Built in 1907, next to E. A. SEEGELKEN'S LIQUOR SALOON (101 Fourth and Wilson) by Batista Bettini on the northwest corner of Fifth and Wilson Streets. An elegant stone building featuring 40 rooms, two dining halls and a bar. It was an extremely busy hotel across from the train station catering to railroad workers and passengers.

In 1911, Bastiste Bettini boasted that the La Rose had a value of $35,000. In 1913, Mansueto Bettini and his wife bought the hotel from his brother Bastista. The hotel was operated from 1935 to 1945 by Rico J. Venturi. Venturi's wife was the daughter of Mansuetto Bettini.

In 1945 the hotel sold to Angelo Seghessi who operated it until 1963. It then sold to William and Pauline Hogan who operated the hotel with their sons Timothy and Paul. The hotel now became an establishment for permanent residents.

As a personal note, I want to express that the hotel became a "low-end" establishment in the 1960's. The Hogan family operated the hotel and is to be admired and remembered for their care to those that stayed at the hotel in the "dark days" of Railroad Square. The Hogan's never refused anyone a meal. They are to be remembered as humanitarians who were a gracious family.

K - 43
La Rose misspelled

HOTEL TORINO

23 West Sixth Street
Bartholomew & John Chiotti – Proprietors 1911
Luigi Rizzi & Paul Pasero – Proprietors 1913

Press Democrat, Number 21, 25 January 1913
DISSOLUTION OF CO-PARTNER-SHIP

The co-partnership existing between Luigi Rizzi and Paul Pasero, doing business under the firm name of The Torino Hotel, situated on Sixth Street, Santa Rosa, Cal., have this day dissolved. Paul Pasero becoming sole proprietor and Luigi Rizzi retiring from the firm. All outstanding accounts against the firm and all accounts due the firm will be settled and collected by Paul Pasero. Signed, Luigi Rizzi, Paul Pasero. Dated Santa Rosa, Jan. 25, 1913.

K - 44

Press Democrat, Number 220, 14 September 1913
ROSSO IS HELD UNDER BONDS PENDING APPEAL

The trial of J. B. Rosso before Judge H. N. N. Latimer, charged with offering ten dollars to M. Sarlglla, Frank De Maria and Tony Gianfranco, of San Francisco, if they would kill Frank Ferrari, was completed Saturday noon. The court put Rosso under bonds and held him over to the Superior Court. Mike Sarlglla and Frank DeMaria, called for the People, testified that they remembered the conversation which took place when the four were together at the **Torino Hotel,** but that Rosso said nothing about Frank Ferrari or anything about paying ten dollars if they would kill him. Rosso testified that he remembered the conversation at that time, and said that no mention was made of Frank Ferrari or anything about paying ten dollars for killing him. The fourth person present, Tony Gianfranco, was the only witness who testified that Rosso made the remark. This witness showed so much interest in the case in whispering to a spectator while upon the witness stand that, upon defendant's motion, the spectator was excluded from the court room during the trial. Both Rosso and Frank Ferrari testified that they were and had always been good friends. Rocco has appealed to the Superior court and released on his own recognizance.

HUMBOLDT SALOON

207 B Street
Edward Kaelin & William J. Hearn Proprietors 1907 - 1911
Anton Rohrer and Louis Gasser Proprietors 1911 –

Press Democrat, Number 175, August 8, 1906
Humboldt Saloon
- Is now open for business at a temporary location on B Street between Fourth and Third Street Ed. Kaelin Proprietor
- The Model **Saloon** Has Temporary Headquarters at 313 A St, Bet. Fourth and Fifth. The Usual Fine Line of Liquor Herman Bayer Proprietor
- John Ritter Walter Schmidt THE GERMANIA SCHMIDT & RITTER Fine Wines, Liquors and Cigars AT THE SAME OLD ,STAND 415 Fourth Street Santa Rosa
- Enterprise **Saloon** THOMAS GEMETTI The Finest of Wines, Liquors and Cigars Third Street, near B

Press Democrat, Number 256, November 2, 1907

> **Notice to the Public**
> Having bought a half interest in the Humboldt Saloon, owned by Ed Kaelin and located on B street. On or about November 1st, we expect to move into our permanent quarters next to Sonoma Market and cordially invite all our friends to come and see us.
> alw   Wm. Hearn.

Press Democrat, Number 260, 1 November 1911
Kaelin Sells Saloon
Ed Kaelin has sold the **Humboldt saloon** on B Street adjoining the Columbia theatre to Anton Rohrer and Louis Gasser. Rohrer has been chief engineer of the Levin Tanning Company, while Gasser is a rancher. The sale was made through the Price & Silvershield agency.

K - 45

JACK'S CLUB
Jack Herron
421 – 4th Street

K – 48

Sorry no information available.

J. M. RONEY

In 1862, at the age of 29, James Madison Roney moved from Pennsylvania to Santa Rosa.

His first venture in Santa Rosa was partnership in the Rialto Saloon on Main Street with William "Billy" Gray. This partnership was formed in February 1862. In August 1862, six months later, Roney and Gray purchased the Oyster Saloon next store to the Rialto. Fen Fisher, the former proprietor of the Oyster Saloon was retained as manager.

In March 1864, Roney and Gray dissolved their partnership with Roney keeping the Oyster Saloon and Gray retaining the Rialto.

In February 1865, Gray sold the Rialto and purchased the Court Saloon on the west side of the plaza. In February 1866, Gray formed a partnership with George Noonan and they purchased the Capitol Saloon. This partnership lasted until 1870.

In February 1871, Roney entered into a partnership with Fred Ablebeck in a wholesale liquor business. This business was named Roney and Ablebeck's Wholesale Liquor House and was located on Main Street.

During this period Ablebeck also owned the Kessing Hotel Billiard Parlor. Ablebeck and Roney dissolved their partnership in August 1872 with Ablebeck returning full time to the Kessing Hotel Billiard Parlor and Roney retaining sole ownership of the wholesale liquor house.

Roney relocated the wholesale house in October 1874 into the old Post Office Building on Fourth Street. His business had expanded into tobacco as well as alcohol.

In April 1875, Peter Prince purchased half interest in Roney's business. The firm was now called Roney and Prince. They were special agents for Hotaling & Co.'s Old Rye, O.K. Whiskey, and A-1 Bourbon Whiskey. They also had an extensive wine trade. This partnership lasted until 1884 when the announced dissolution of the business and closed.

In 1886, Roney opened the Santa Rosa Wine Vaults and also was the agent for Union Ice Company. The business was located at 507 Fourth Street until Roney's death in 1893.

RONEY & PRINCE
505 - 507 Fourth Street
James Madison Roney Proprietor
1874 – 1885
W. Smith – Sales person
Peter Prince Proprietor
1875 – 1885

SANTA ROSA WINE VAULTS
507 Fourth Street
James Madison Roney Proprietor
1886 - 1893

RONEY & PRINCE PAPER LABEL

J. M. RONEY

Size:	Half Pint
Style:	Pumpkinseed
Year:	1900
Height:	5¼ Inches Tall
Type Top:	Tooled
Color:	Clear
Bottom:	Blank
Rarity:	Semi Common

**J. M. RONEY
WHOLESALE
LIQUORS
SANTA ROSA**

J. M. RONEY

Size: Half Pint
Style: Pumpkinseed
Year: 1900
Height: 5¾ Inches Tall
Type Top: Tooled
Color: Clear
Bottom: Blank
Rarity: Semi Common

**J. M. RONEY
WHOLESALE
LIQUORS
SANTA ROSA**

J. M. RONEY

Size: Pint
Style: Pumpkinseed
Year: 1900
Height: 6½ Inches Tall
Type Top: Tooled
Color: Clear
Bottom: Blank
Rarity: Semi Common

**J. M. RONEY
WHOLESALE
LIQUORS
SANTA ROSA**

J. M. RONEY

Size:	Pint
Style:	Flask
Year:	1900
Height:	????? Inches Tall
Type Top:	Tooled
Color:	Clear
Bottom:	Blank
Rarity:	Extremely Rare

Line drawing John Thomas Book

**J. M. RONEY
WHOLESALE
LIQUORS
SANTA ROSA**

JONES & MATHEWS SALOON

531 – Fourth Street
Walter Jones Proprietor – 1908 - 1918
John Mathews Proprietor - 1908 - 1910

J & M Saloon stood for Walter Jones and John Mathews. Their partnership dissolved in 1910 when Mathews sold his interest. The saloon remained in the same location at 531 - 4th Street until 1918 when it closed because of Prohibition.

There are two different size pumpkin-seeds of the same design with one being 5" tall and the other 6½" tall. Both are clear glass with tooled top.

**JONES & MATHEWS
SANTA ROSA**

Size:	Half Pint
Style:	Pumpkinseed
Year:	1900
Height:	5 Inches Tall
Type Top:	Tooled
Color:	Clear
Bottom:	1213
Rarity:	Extremely Rare

Size:	Pint
Style:	Pumpkinseed
Year:	1900
Height:	6½ Inches Tall
Type Top:	Tooled
Color:	Clear
Bottom:	1079
Rarity:	Extremely Rare

**JONES & MATHEWS
SANTA ROSA**

Line drawings from John Thomas book.

JONES & MATHEWS

Size:	Half pint
Style:	Coffin
Year:	1900
Height:	6"
Type Top:	Tooled
Color:	Clear
Bottom:	#1079
Rarity:	Extremely Rare

**JONES & MATHEWS
SANTA ROSA**

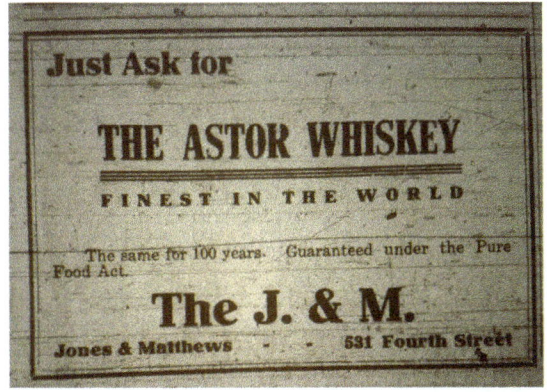

JONES & MATHEWS

Size:	Pint
Style:	Coffin
Year:	1900
Height:	7½ "
Type Top:	Tooled
Color:	Clear
Bottom:	#1213
Rarity:	Extremely Rare

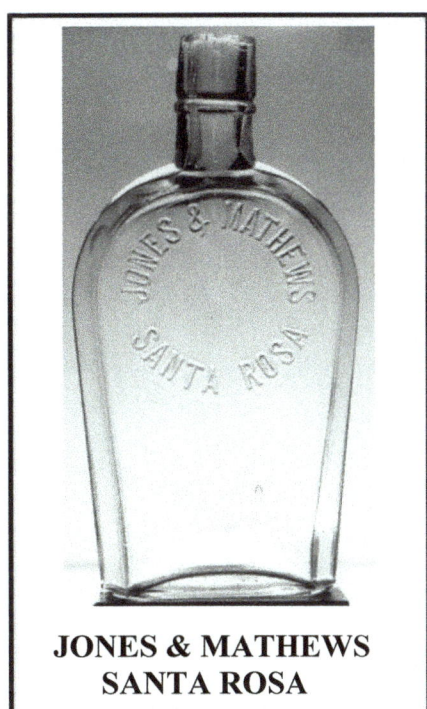

**JONES & MATHEWS
SANTA ROSA**

LODGE SALOON

J. J. Krawetzki Proprietor
Charles J. Krause – Proprietor 1904

Press Democrat, Number 232, September 30, 1904
Purchases Business Property

Through the agency of Capt. Guy E, Groose, the saloon property at the corner of Second and Main streets belonging to J. J. Krawetzki has been sold to Charles J. Krause, who will fix it up in first-class style and conduct the business in future. The properly is sometimes known as the old Jack Atkins corner, and the lot is 40x 120 in size. The price at, which the property changed hands is said to have been $6,000.

K – 61

MILANO SALOON (U. S. Saloon)
(1909 – 1910)
123-4 Fourth Street
J. Ambrose Perotta & Peter Girolo – Proprietors

Press Democrat, Number 80, April 3, 1907
The license for the old **Milano hotel** on lower Fourth Street was denied.

Press Democrat, Number 96, 21 April 1907

ARREST UNDER NEW Of ORDINANCE
Eliza Perotta Charged With Violation of Probation for the New Restaurant Licensee

Eliza Perotta, the erstwhile former proprietor of the **Milano hotel** on lower Fourth street, who lost his license for disobeying the city ordinance some time ago, and who since opened a restaurant, is again In trouble. A complaint was sworn out by Police Officer John M. Boyes on Saturday against Perotta charging her with a violation of the new license ordinance No. 238, particularly the section applying to restaurant licenses. It was stated that three men went Into Perotta's restaurant and three drinks were put on a table and at the same time a plate with two or three crackers on it was also placed thereon. The restaurant ordinance provides that liquors can be served with meals only, and the cracker diet is not going to be tolerated and in this instance the arresting officer, knew it was only a "blind."

Press Democrat, Number 116, May 17, 1907
Mrs. Perotta Fined Again
Eliza Perotta was fined $20 by Judge Bagley for violating the restaurant license at the old **Milano hotel** on lower Fourth Street. This is twice her has 'been fined within a month. Police Officer Ed Skaggs made the arrest.

K - 64

Press Democrat, Number 276, November 19, 1911
1400 IS SEEN FROM A SALOON
Bold Robbery of the U. S. Bar on Lower Fourth Street on Saturday Morning

MILANO SALOON (U. S. Saloon)

A thief extracted a sack containing money front a drawer back of the bar In the U. S. saloon on lower Fourth Street sometime Saturday, between half past ten o'clock in the morning and one o'clock in the afternoon. The identity of the thief is as mysterious as the disappearance of the coin. The saloon is run by Perotta & Girolo. On Saturdays they have been in the habit of cashing a good many small checks for working men who visit the place. Saturday morning Perotta went to San Francisco, but before his departure brought the money to the saloon and put in the drawer so that it would be ready for Girolo to cash checks when presented. Girolo went to the sack about half past ten and gave change for a ten dollar gold piece with two fives. That is the last he saw of the sack. Saturday afternoon at one o'clock he went to the drawer again to cash a check and found the sack gone. The police spent the afternoon and Saturday night investigating, but the thief could not be found. No one knows who he is, and as the money was in coin it will be pretty hard to locate the guilty party.

NEW CORNER

HUDSON & McKee LIQUOR SALOON
(New Corner)
20 Main Street
W. H. Hudson & Sam McKee – Co-proprietors - ??? - 1909
John White & Son Proprietors – 1909 - 1916

Press Democrat, Number 16, January 20, 1909
Tie Vote on License In the matter of McKee & Hudson's application for a retail liquor license for their place on Main Street. Attorney H. W. A. Weske appeared, and explained the situation. A roll call was ordered, and the vote stood three for and three against, thus 'passing it up" to - Mayor Gray. The Mayor said he was not going to vote until he had looked into the matter as to whether the people in the vicinity wanted the saloon or not.

Councilmen Barham, Bronson and Johnston voted for the license, and Councilmen Burris. Steiner and Forgett voted against it. Councilman Burris said Santa Rosa had enough saloons already. Councilman Barham said it was the last saloon license he would vote for; after this he would vote to decrease the number.

Press Democrat, Number 295, 18 December 1912
COUNCIL REFUSE THREE LICENSES
The three applications denied renewal was as follows: Ferrari and Moranda, 113 Fourth street; **Hudson & McKee, 20 Main Street**;

Press Democrat, Number 5, 7 January 1909
Will Have Corner Grocery: John White and son.
John C. White, has purchased the saloon business of Sam McKee at Main and First Street, and is making a number of improvements in the place. They are planning to put in a stock of groceries, and run the bar in connection with the store, although in another room.

NORTHWESTERN LIQUOR STORE

(Enterprise Saloon)
By Gaye LeBaron
Published in the Press Democrat
December 11, 1983

In the 1924 Santa Rosa directory, Thomas Gemetti is listed as "Proprietor, Soft Drink Parlor." If you believe that, I've got some Grace Brothers Beer stock to sell you. Cheap.

There was lots of money made selling "soft drinks" here between 1920 and 1933 - more money, by far, than one would expect from the bottles of soda pop that passed over the counters of a half-hundred Sonoma County saloons.

The reason for this profit inflation, of course, was the fact that the sale of alcoholic beverages did not cease with Prohibition. The choice of brands may have been limited, but for those who knew their way around the county, the whiskey was available. And the wine. And the beer.

The noble experiment ended 50 years ago this week. To the sound of glasses clinking. But, then, the glasses had never stopped clinking during the years that the United States was "dry." Some of these clinks were necessarily muffled as a new word was added to the lexicon of American English - "speakeasy." Derived from the need to keep voices hushed to avoid detection, the word meant a place where people went to obtain illegal liquor.

Traditional "speaks" were few in Sonoma County, not because there was no drinking but because they were primarily big city establishments, special places, often in basements, sometimes with entertainment, some run by mobsters. Sonoma County residents weren't that sophisticated. They did their illegal drinking in roadhouses, old country homes converted for the purpose, or in hotels and saloons that never stopped selling booze.

One of these was Tom Gemetti's saloon on Third Street. Opened at the turn of the century by a Swiss-Italian immigrant who started a bakery shop and switched to stronger stuff, Gemetti's sold liquor to Santa Rosans and to the farmers when they were in town, before, after and DURING, Prohibition.

It wasn't unique in this aspect; there were half a dozen places in town doing likewise, a like amount in Petaluma, plus several in Healdsburg, Guerneville and Occidental. What was unique about Gemetti's was that it was NEVER closed down - not by the local authorities, not by the Feds.

Tom Gemetti's daughters-in-law, Beatrice and Esther, recall that he was very proud of the fact that there "was never any trouble at Gemetti's."

"He was very particular about the way he ran the place," Beatrice Gemetti recalls. "And proud of the fact that all the men on the police department were his friends."

That may have been part of the reason for his uninterrupted commerce. Says Esther Gemetti, widow of Tom's son Elvin, who ran Gemetti's after Repeal: "My husband always said that the police force, the judges, and the lawyers were his father's best customers."
He never offered them bribes or anything," says Beatrice. "They were just his friends."

Old Tom Gemetti had lots of friends. The picture that emerges of his saloon is one of a "family" establishment. "The old families from up the coast, around Gualala, the Nonellas and the others, they were all friends and when they came to town, they stopped in," says Beatrice.
Esther recalls that his sphere of influence extended into Western Marin. "All the Swiss-Italians, from down around Tomales and that way," came to rub elbows with Santa Rosa merchants AND lawyers AND police AND judges.

A Saturday afternoon at Gemetti's was a social event. There were card tables at the back of the saloon. "They didn't play for money," says Esther. "They played for chips. And there were a slot machines for a while when that was legal (post-Repeal), but not for long."

It was more than a saloon. "When people needed money, they went to Tom Gemetti," Beatrice recalls. And he looked after their valuables. "He had a big old safe in the saloon," Beatrice says, "full of little cupboards like safe deposit boxes. We took it to the store (her late husband, Fred Gemetti, owned a feed store) and found that some of them were still locked. They were full of old papers and things he was keeping safe for people and they never picked them up."

Part of Tom's success in running a "clean" establishment he attributed to purity of gender. There were NO women allowed in Gemetti's. "He was very fussy" Esther remembers, "I was never inside the saloon. My husband wouldn't allow it - until the telephone company came in."

When Pacific Telephone built offices next store, Gemetti's remodeled, "about 48 years ago," Esther thinks and they built "booths in front so the operators could have lunch." Lunch was 25 cents, all you could eat. "After that," says Esther, "I could go in front, where the ice cream was, but I was never in back, in the saloon."

Gemetti's was torn down in 1954 when the building was sold to the phone company for expansion of its headquarters here. That was the first time it was closed.

Other establishments that survived Prohibition could not claim such a record. Federal agents closed down the Buon Gusto (now Lena's), the Hotel D'Italia across the street and the Toscano (now Michele's) with regularity. They pleaded guilty, paid their fines and were open for business again within a week.

Such was the case with Buffi's Depot Hotel in Healdsburg, with Jake Luppold's Main Street saloon, with Gnesa's on Fourth Street, with a bar called the Oberon in downtown Santa Rosa, with the Garibaldi Hotel in Guerneville, the Toscano in Sonoma, the Altamont and the Union and the Golden Gate in Occidental. It was like paying dues.

Every road headed out of town had a stopping place. They usually had a watertrough Raford Leggett recalls, careful to point out that "I didn't frequent them, of course. You needed a password and I was just a country boy."

"Stopping to water the horses," was an excuse as well as a euphemism for imbibing, maybe at Giacomini's Corners at the big turn in the Sebastopol Road, or Lalolie's, east of town, or a couple of places with French names in El Verano, or Emma Fetter's hotel at the hot springs.

There was a "spot going north, just about where the round barn is," Leggett recalls. Bob Whiting, another old timer, remembers Smith's Corners, west of town on Sebastopol Road. Some Petaluman's talk about a place called Queenie's on the I Street extension and a big house high on the Lichau Road hill. But Petaluma's old-timers are loath to confirm these rumors. Fifty years, in Petaluma, is not long enough.
In the first week of December, 1933, it ended. Utah became the 36th state to ratify the repeal of the 18th amendment to the Constitution and the Volstead Act, prohibiting the sale of alcohol, was declared void.

President Roosevelt announced the news with a plea to citizens to help "restore law and order." That task was made much simpler by the fact that drinking was now legal. But nothing is perfect. On December 9th, a Press Democrat reported wrote that "Santa Rosa was as dry as the Sahara desert last night, as far as being able to buy a drink." The new liquor laws that accompanied repeal, requiring sellers to be licensed and to have tax stamps on their bottles, frightened the sellers. "Get legal or get out" was the advice of federal authorities. Thus, the temporary lull in nightspots, while they made necessary arrangements.

Bottles of familiar brands like Old Crow, Four Roses and Old Granddad began to appear on the back bars along with some more exotic containers as William Shackleton, district administrator for the Board of Equalization on the North Coast announced that even bootleggers would be allowed to buy tax stamps for their products.

Ransom Cook, described in the Press Democrat as a "local banker" (he was later the head of the mighty Bank of America), gave a humorous speech at the Rotary Club called "Reactions of a Dry" while WCTU members - "an earnest group." the newspaper called them - held an all-day meeting at the Baptist Church to "outline new goals."

I doubt if total Prohibition was among them. It seemed evident that the citizens of the U.S.A. were not about to try THAT again.

Thank You Gaye……………………………

NORTHWESTERN LIQUOR STORE

GEMETTI'S – 516 - 3rd STREET

BUSINESS CARDS

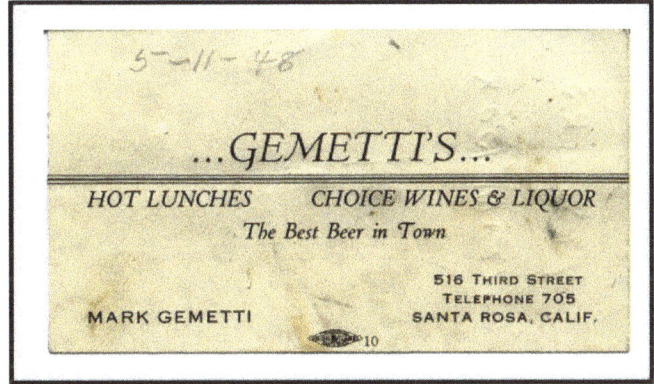

NORTHWESTERN LIQUOR STORE

NORTHWESTERN LIQUOR STORE
Thos. Gemetti, Prop.
Santa Rosa, Cal.

Pumpkinseed
Tooled top
Paper Label
6¾ Inches tall
Clear glass
Rarity: Rare

J. F. CUTTER
BLENDED
BOURBON
BOTTLED BY
THOS. GEMETTI
SANTA ROSA, CAL.
NET CONTENTS 10 OZS.

NORTHWESTERN LIQUOR STORE

Picnic flask
Screw top
6¼ Inches tall
Clear glass
Rarity: Rare

**NORTHWESTERN
LIQUOR STORE
THOS. GEMETTI
SANTA ROSA, CAL.**

Picnic flask
Screw top
6¾ Inches tall
Clear glass
Rarity: Rare

**NORTHWESTERN
LIQUOR STORE
THOS. GEMETTI
SANTA ROSA, CAL.**

NORTHWESTERN LIQUOR STORE

ENTERPRISE SALOON
Third Street near B Street - Thomas Gemetti proprietor 1906

K – 36 Large 5c   **K – 37 Small 5 – No c**

K – 38 – Small GEMETTI'S without comma after "STREET"

K – 39 – Large GEMETTI'S with comma after "STREET"

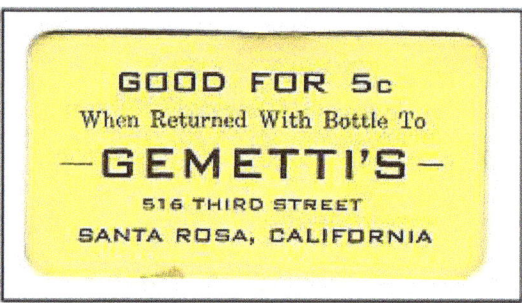

Gemetti's Card Board Token

NORTHWESTERN LIQUOR STORE

GEMETTI'S - NORTHWESTERN
LIQUOR STORE PAPER LABELS

GILT EDGE

OLD CROW

NORTHWESTERN LIQUOR STORE

NELSON 1903 WHISKEY

PONY EXTRA SPECIAL

NORTHWESTERN LIQUOR STORE

S. B. ROSS BLEND WHISKY

OLD PRENTICE WHISKY

NORTHWESTERN LIQUOR STORE

NONPAREIL O. P. S. HIGH GRADE **ATHERTON FINE OLD WHISKEY**

Gemetti's
Bar Special
90 Proof
Straight Bourbon Whiskey

Bottled for
GEMETTI BROS.
Santa Rosa, California

Mark Silva Bottle

OCCIDENTAL HOTEL

Robert McGeorge
443 Fourth Street

George A. Tupper – Proprietor
443 Fourth Street
W. W. Waite - Bar Keeper

George A. Tupper built this first class hotel in Santa Rosa in 1876. Born in Macomb County, Michigan, November 27, 1833, he arrived in San Francisco in November 1852 when he was 19 years old. In 1856, he arrived in Sonoma County and started farming five miles south of Santa Rosa on Petaluma Road. In 1862, he moved into downtown Santa Rosa and opened a general store that he operated until 1876.

In 1876, he then built and operated the elegant Occidental Hotel; a three-story brick building that housed 150 rooms, and then sold the hotel in 1878. He then repurchased the hotel in December 1879, an operated it until 1900 when it was sold to Frank Bane and Patrick Quinn.

Like brick other buildings in downtown Santa Rosa, it was destroyed in the 1906 earthquake. At the time it was still under the ownership of Frank Bane and Patrick Quinn. The hotel was rebuilt into a two-story hotel after the earthquake.

Quinn died in _____ and Charles and J. Russell Banes joined their brother Frank as partners. In 1915, Leonard Howarth, at the time one of Santa Rosa's most influential citizens and among the wealthiest men in the State of California, purchased the hotel. In the mid-1930's, Howarth added a third story to the hotel expanding it to 150 rooms once again.

Howarth died a multi-millionaire on May 12, 1930 and the hotel went to his only heirs, his nieces, Ada Pilz, Ellen Howarth Moody and Lillian Meadowcroft.

In November, 1951, Fred Rosenberg purchased the hotel from Howarth's nieces and later the same month leased the hotel to R. L. Kronstedt and his son Jack Kronstedt. In October, 1962, the Kronstedt's sold their lease to Fisher Hotels.

Early business card

OCCIDENTAL HOTEL

K - 69

Postcard

F. O. REEDER

K -81
Reeder had a cigar stand in the Occidental Hotel.

OLD CORNER

Corners Second & Main Streets
W. S. Seegelken – Proprietor - 1904
Charles Krause – Proprietor – 1906

OLD CORNER SALOON (1905)
Corners Second & Main Streets
W. S. Seegelken – Proprietor

OLD CORNER SALOON (1906 – 1910)
Corners Second & Main Streets
Charles Krause - Proprietor

SONOMA COUNTY LIBRARY PHOTO

K – 164

K - 73

K - 74

Unlisted

"O. K." SALOON

201 Fourth Street
S. Rossi Proprietor 1899
Joseph Cavagna & Battiste Fenaci – Proprietors 1899 - 1911

Press Democrat, Number 79, 8 July 1899
The "O. K." Has Changed Hands

The **O. K, saloon** at 201 Fourth Street has changed hands S. Rossi having sold the place to Messrs. Fenaci & Cavagna. Both the new proprietors are well and favorably known in Santa Rosa, Mr. Fenaci having been the head cook at the Campi restaurant in this city for some years.

Press Democrat, Number 211, 25 August 1905
S. Rossi, formerly proprietor of the **O. K. saloon** here, was in town on Thursday from Petaluma where he is residing.

K - 72

PALACE LIQUOR SALOON

W. B. Morris – Proprietor 1878 – 1883
DeFreest & Allison – Proprietors 1883 - 1901
Jesse Brunk and George Brittain – Proprietors 1901 - 1902
Len Brittain & Jesse Z. Brunk Proprietors 1902 – 1902
Harvey Brittain & Jesse Z. Brunk Proprietors 1902 - 1909
546 3rd Street

Press Democrat, Number 34, December 11, 1883
Notice:
We (DeFreest & Allison) wish to inform the public that we have purchased the interest of W. B. Morris in the **PALACE SALOON** and intend to run it as a FIRST-GLASS HOUSE In every particular, our specialty being " FINE WINES, GOOD LIQUORS and prompt and polite attention on shortest notice. Pool tables and everything needed therewith, always in perfect order. We would like to call attention to our J. H. CUTTER WHISKEY, of which we have received a consign merit. This popular brand speaks for itself, and needs no comment on our part. Our Cigars are chosen from among some of the most select brands, and we guarantee to give perfect satisfaction. The **Palace Saloon,** having recently undergone considerable alterations and improvements, is at present the best arranged and finest **saloon** in Sonoma County. Fredericksburg beer is on draught.

Press Democrat, Number 9, October 22, 1901
Bought Out the Palace Saloon
Jesse Brunk and George Brittain bought out the **"Palace" saloon** on Monday from Lindsay B. Cheatham and intend to run the same. Mr.' Cheatham or rather First Lieutenant Cheatham of the Philippine Scouts, as he is now known leaves shortly for his post of duty in the Philippines.

Press Democrat, Number 111, 20 February 1902
George Brittain Bails Out
George Brittain, who has been a partner with Jesse Brunk, in the **Palace saloon** at 3rd and Main Streets, has sold interest to his brother, Harvey Brittain, who with Mr. Brunk will conduct the business In the future. Harvey has a large circle of friends In Santa Rosa, who wish him success. Harry Wolf has accepted the position of barkeeper, and his genial smile and happy manner has been transferred from Fourth to Third Street, where he says he will be glad to meet his old friends.

Press Democrat, Number 185, May 17, 1902
Case Set for Trial
The case against J. Brunk of the **Palace saloon,** charged with a violation of a city ordinance regarding alleged gaming in his place of business, was yesterday set down for trial for May 22d by Police Judge Bagley.

PALACE LIQUOR SALOON

Press Democrat, Number 192, May 25, 1902
Len Brittain, who recently returned to this city from Crockett, has purchased the interest formerly held by his brother, Harvey Brittain, in the **Palace Saloon** at the corner of Third and Main Streets, and will in future he associated with Jesse Brunk in the conduct of the same

Picnic flask
Twist top
6¼" Inches tall
Clear glass
Paper label
#1225 on bottom base
Rarity: Rare

**CEDAR BROOK
FORMERLY
? H McBRAYER
LAWRENCEBURG, KY.
BOTTLED BY
THE PALACE
BRITTAIN & BRUNK, Props.
Santa Rosa, Calif.**

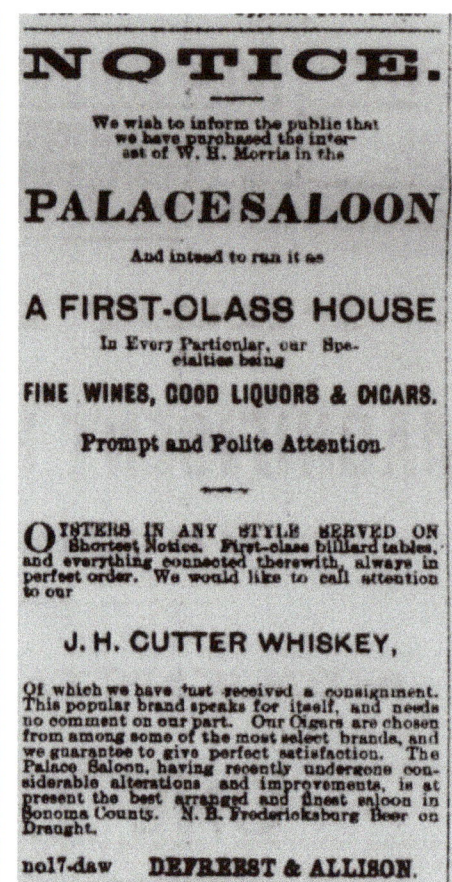

K - 65

PEERLESS SALOON

518 Fourth Street
Hearn & Sweeny Proprietors
Ed M. Nelson Proprietor 1902 – 1903
Calhoun & McKee Proprietors 1903 – 1904
McKee Proprietor 1904 - 1909

Press Democrat, Number 219, 27 June 1902

Press Democrat, Number 35, November 26, 1902
Opening of "The Peerless"
This evening there will be a grand opening at "The Peerless" saloon at 518 Fourth Street, when the new proprietor, Ed M. Nelson, will welcome his friends

Press Democrat, Number 106, February 18, 1903
Calhoun & McKee were granted a retail liquor license for the Peerless saloon on Fourth Street. The committee of investigation was Councilmen Brown, Johnson and King.

Press Democrat, Number 105, May 5, 1904
Landlord McKee of the Peerless saloon on Fourth Street has had an elegant piece of furniture placed in his establishment. It is a bar made out of oak. The work was carried out by Simpson & Roberts.

Press Democrat, Number 148, June 24, 1904
Some Neat Improvements
The old Peerless Saloon has, under the new management of McKee & Co., been entirely remodeled. The place will be formally opened on Saturday night. Instead of the old side bar, which has been abandoned, a new one has been put in which is made in the shape of a horseshoe The bar is made of oak and it Is grained and polished in imitation of the original oak, A handsome ice chest and refrigerator with plate glass mirrors is filled up behind the bar. A barber shop is also one of the attractions.

SANTA ROSA

PEERLESS SALOON

Press Democrat, Number 145, June 20, 1907
VIOLATED A CITY ORDINANCE
Wednesday night about half-past 10 o'clock Police Officer Lindley arrested a woman whom he noticed leaving McKee & Morrison's saloon on Fifth street. Under the ordinance no woman or minors are allowed to frequent a saloon. The woman was taken to the police station and put up twenty dollars bail for her appearance before Police Judge Bagley. She claims to have been in the saloon for the purpose of getting some washing.

Press Democrat, Number 148, June 24, 1904
Everybody and their friends are invited to the opening of the "**Horseshoe.**" **saloon, formerly the Peerless,** Saturday night, July 25th. All will be treated well and will leave well satisfied.

Unlisted – A   **Unlisted - B**

ROYAL SALOON

536 Third Street
Neal Gillooly – Proprietor

Becomes Quinlan's in 1905
Dan & Mary Quinlan Proprietors

Becomes Jesse Daws Saloon 1913
Jesse Daw Proprietor

Press Democrat, Number 20 December 17, 1898
There will be a grand opening of the Royal saloon, 536 Third Street, Saturday evening. N. Gillooly is the new proprietor.

K - 154

QUINLAN'S SALOON

Press Democrat, Number 36, 11 February 1905
Opening Saturday Night
Dan Quinlan, who has purchased the Royal saloon at 536 Third Street, will give an opening Saturday night, February 11, to which he invites his friends and the public in general.

Press Democrat, Number 216, 9 September 1913
Will Sell Saloon Contents
As will be seen by an advertisement in another column of this morning's paper, permission has been granted in the estate of Daniel Quinlan to sell the contents of the old Quinlan saloon on Third Street. D. R. Gale is the attorney for the administration of the estate.

Press Democrat, Number 257, 28 October 1913
Jesse Daw Buys Saloon
Mary E. Quinlan, as administrator of the estate of her late husband. Dan Quinlan has sold the contents of the Royal Saloon, 136 Third Street, to Jesse W. Daw, who is to take possession on November 3.

Press Democrat, Number 220, 14 September 1913

NOTICE OF SALE OF PERSONAL PROPERTY—In the Superior Court of the State of California, in and for the County of Sonoma. In the Matter of the Estate of Daniel F. Quinlan, deceased.

Notice is hereby given that in pursuance of an order of the Superior Court of the County of Sonoma, State of California, made on the 8th day of September, 1913, in the matter of the estate of Daniel F. Quinlan, deceased, the undersigned administratrix of the estate of said deceased, will sell at private sale to the highest and best bidder for cash, gold coin of the United States, on or after Monday, the 15th day of September, 1913, at eleven o'clock A. M., at the Royal Saloon, No. 536 Third Street, Santa Rosa, California, the following personal property, to-wit: All the stock and stocks of wines and other liquors contained and located in said Royal Saloon, and also the following other personal property contained in said saloon: 9 dozen glasses, one table, 7 chairs, one iron safe, one front bar and one back bar and foot rail, two gas plates and one range, one cash register, two vases and one glass tray.

MARY E. QUINLAN,
Administratrix of the Estate of Daniel F. Quinlan, deceased.
D. R. Gale, attorney for said estate.
Dated, September 9th, 1913. a-9-15

Quinlan Pocket Mirrors

JESSE W. DAW

Press Democrat, Number 257, 28 October 1913
Jesse Daw Buys Saloon Mary E. Quinlan, as administrator of the estate of her late husband. Dan Quinlan has sold the contents of the Royal Saloon, 536 Third Street, to Jesse W. Daw, who is to take possession on November 3rd.

K - 120

SAMPLE ROOM

524 Fourth Street
Louis Blum & Jacob Blum Proprietor's 1889 – 1906

Press Democrat, Number 35, February 8, 1899
New Sample Rooms
Louis Blum has opened his neat and cozy little drinking place on Fourth Street in the rear of the Savings bank, and calls it the "Sample Room." It has been fitted up very nicely throughout and stocked with the very best brands of liquor.

Press Democrat, Number 231, 16 July 1903
Sample and Billiard Rooms 524 Fourth St. 221 Exchange is where you get the Finest Drinks In the City
Blum * Blum Proprietor

Press Democrat, Number 239, 7 December 1904
BLUM'S SAMPLE & BILLIARD ROOMS 524 Fourth St, 22 Exchange Avenue is where you get the Finest Drinks in the City. Liquors are the Very Best. Cozy Card Rooms. **Blum & Blum.** Proprietor

K – 157

K – 158

K – 159

SANTA ROSA HOUSE

(Colgan's Hotel – 1854)

Edward Colgan, born July 30, 1823 in New York, arrived in California via Cape Horn in time to experience the 1849 Gold Rush. He opened a restaurant in San Francisco and operated it until he was driven out of business by the floods.

On October 12, 1853, being an adventurous 30 year old, he relocated in Santa Rosa. In 1854 the first Masonic Building in Santa Rosa, a two-story building was completed, and Colgan leased the ground floor and converted it into a hotel. This was the third public building in Santa Rosa at the time.

He opened the first hotel in Santa Rosa, The Santa Rosa House, a two-story white wood-framed building with seven columns with an upstairs porch, on the corner of First and Main (now Santa Rosa Avenue). On the ground floor Wells Fargo Express Station had an office with the hotel being upstairs on the second floor. Through the years Colgan continued to add additional rooms and the hotel became the largest public building in the county.

The railroad came to Santa Rosa in 1872 and the hotel was successful as Colgan would transport passengers from the railroad to his hotel. Colgan operated the hotel until his death July, 1876. His wife continued to operate the hotel until it closed on September 23, 1881.

Colgan's son, Edward Power Colgan, Jr. became the county sheriff in 1886 and state controller in 1890. His other son, Lincoln Colgan, converted the original hotel into a laundry and then a blacksmith shop. The blacksmith shop was passed to George Colgan (Lincoln's son) in later years. In the 1920's the building was raised and moved back several yards on the property to make way for a service station. The dilapidated building was torn down in the 1940's.

Cogan's housed the **EXCHANGE SALOON** and the address listed for the saloon was 21 Exchange Avenue.

EXCHANGE SALOON (Court Exchange)
21 Exchange Avenue
Giles G. Youker – Proprietor – 1878 -1885
Smith - Proprietor - 1878 - 1875
Thomas E. Monroe - Bar Keeper
William Kohle - Bar Keeper

COURT EXCHANGE SALOON
(Formerly Exchange Saloon)
Edward R. C. Nagle – Proprietor - 1885

EXCHANGE SALOON
(Court Exchange Sample Room)
21 Exchange Avenue
Press M. Hall - Proprietor - 1886

EXCHANGE SALOON
(Court Exchange Sample Room)
21 Exchange Avenue
Press M. Hall - Proprietor - 1887

COURT EXCHANGE OYSTER SALOON TRADE CARD

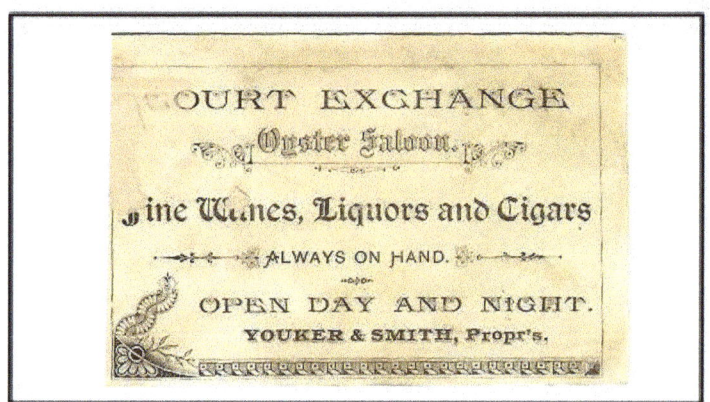

SECOND CLASS SALOON

W. A. Ford & Meador Proprietors - ? 1908
W. J. Hearn & A. J. Caughey Proprietors – 1908 – 1909
W. J. Hearn Proprietor – 1909 -

Officer Nick Yeager addressed the Council regarding the trouble at Ford & Meador's saloon Monday night, when the proprietors were both placed under arrest with two other men, and fined yesterday. Ford was drunk and using foul language on the street, he said, and when he arrested him Meador and others Interfered and took him into the saloon, from where he was later removed to the police station and released on ball. Ford was given an opportunity to speak for himself and tried to pass the matter off lightly by admitting that he was drunk and could not remember what had occurred, but declared that other saloon men had done us bad without losing their licenses. He was informed that any further offense would result in the revoking of his license.

Press Democrat, Number 113, May 13, 1908
THREE HERE ARE FIRED, SQUEALED ARREST
W. A. Ford, one of the proprietors of the" second class" saloon at Fourth and a Streets, was fined $20 for disturbing the peace and $5 dollars for being drunk by city recorder Bagley yesterday as a result of the trouble Monday night at which time he was arrested by Officer Yeager. His partner Bert Meador was fined $10 for disturbing the peace as was William Moss, on a similar charge. They both brought the trouble on themselves for interfering when Ford was placed under arrest.

Press Democrat, Number 200, August 22, 1908
Change of Proprietor
Messrs. Hearn & Caughey have purchased the Second Class Saloon of **Ford & Meador,** corner Fourth and Washington streets. All bills owing to the latter firm are payable to them and all accounts against them will be settled by them. Hearn & Caughey. Dated August 18, 1908

Press Democrat, Number 237, October 10, 1909
Has Purchased the Louvre
W. J. **Hearn** has purchased the Interest of A. J. **Caughey** in the Louvre and will pay all bills and receive all monies due.

Unlisted – Small 5c - Cigar   **Unlisted – Large 5 - In Trade**

SENATE SALOON

SENATE SALOON
2nd & Main Street (Same old place)
Jake Luppold - Proprietor

K – 92

K – 92 A

K – 92 B

SENATE SALOON

Press Democrat, Number 293, November 30, 1905
"THE SENATE" SALOON Handsome Resort on Main Street Conducted by Jacob Luppold

Four years ago Jacob Luppold bought the saloon at 103 Main Street, and rechristened it "The Senate." Then he set about improving the appearance of the place in every way of which he could think. The first embellishment was a handsome new front, ornamented with panel designs by an artist in oils. Then he got the notion that the back was not in keeping with the front, so he had the old bar and sideboard torn out and replaced by the finest creations of a skilled local artisan in native woods —curly redwood and burl. New furniture bad to follow this, and cozy card rooms were partitioned off from the main room. Now it is one of the finest bars in town. The plate-glass mirror reflects the gleam of new chandeliers; there are plenty of comfortable chairs. The latest magazines and papers are always within reach, and a real good free lunch is at hand. The appearance of the place is not all that has received the proprietor's careful attention. He is himself a connoisseur in liquids and he knows the best. He does not claim to have all the good liquor in town or the only good liquor in town. But he has none that is poor. In distilled liquors his specialty is straight goods, but he keeps a small line of blended whiskies as well. There is a full line of wines. He makes a leader of Grace Brothers' beers, but if you want St. Louis beer he has the A. B. C. and Lemp's; also he has Fredericksburg in bottles. Frank Cootes is Luppold's head bartender. He is away up in the business, just the same as Luppold. Either of them can serve you to the Queen's taste.

Press Democrat, Number 230, 13 November 1909
LUPPOLD BUYS THE SPEEDLING
A deal has been consummated, whereby J. J. Luppold, former proprietor of The Senate, on Main street, has purchased the saloon at Gwinn s Corners, from Mr. Speedling. He will take possession at once. The "Mayor of Main Street'' has many friends and he expects to do a big business. Mr. and Mrs. Speedling have not fully determined their future plans.

THE MODEL SALOON
SANTA ROSA, CALIFORNIA

In 1880 a man whose last name is Gillard opened the Model Saloon at 540 Fourth Street. The business was sold 1883 to the Groshong brothers then to in Enoch Yates in 1885. John J. Daly was a bartender with Yates. Herman Bayer purchased the Model in 1890.

Bayer was a native of Germany, born near Osnabruech on March 25, 1860. He was president of Santa Rosa Lodge of the Royal Arch, vice-president of Santa Rosa Lodge No. 25, Order of Hermann Sons, and he was also a member of the Aerie of Eagles, Santa Rosa Grove of Druids, and Santa Rosa Court of the Foresters of America. He was also a member of the German Glee Club. He had become one of the most popular Santa Rosa citizens.

THE MODEL LIQUOR SALOON
540 Fourth Street
Gillard Proprietor   (1880)

THE MODEL LIQUOR SALOON
Groshong Bros.   (1883)
541 – Fourth Street

MODEL LIQUOR SALOON
540 Fourth Street
Enoch Yates – Proprietor   (1885 – 1890)
John J. Daly - Bar Keeper

MODEL LIQUOR SALOON
313 A Street between Fourth & Fifth Streets (Temporary Headquarters)
Herman Bayer - Proprietor   (1890 - 1910)
Bayer had been tending bar at the New York Hotel from 1887 until he purchased the Model Liquor saloon in 1890. Charles Wolf was the proprietor of the New York Hotel located at the corner of Fourth & Davis Streets.

Sonoma Index-Tribune – August 10, 1910
HERMAN BAYER WAS A VICTIM
Was one of the Twelve Killed in Train Wreck near Ignacio

One of the victims of the terrible railroad catastrophe on the Northwestern Pacific near Ignacio, last Monday evening, was Herman Bayer the well-known proprietor of the Model saloon, Santa Rosa. When the unfortunate man met his death he was seated in the smoker and was instantly killed by an iron rod entering his mouth and penetrating his head. Seated beside him when he met his fate was Dr. Watson who was one of the few in the smoker who escaped death or serious injury. Instantly after the collision the smoker-car was converted into a veritable human slaughter pen. Here it was that the twelve victims met their fate in a most horrible manner.

MODEL LIQUOR SALOON
543 Fourth Street
Herman Bayer estate   (1911)

MODEL LIQUOR SALOON
543 Fourth Street
R. R. O'Brien – Proprietor   (1911)

THE MODEL

Size:	Half Pint
Style:	Coffin
Year:	1900/10
Height:	6 Inches Tall
Type Top:	Tooled
Color:	Amethyst
Bottom:	1079
Rarity:	Rare

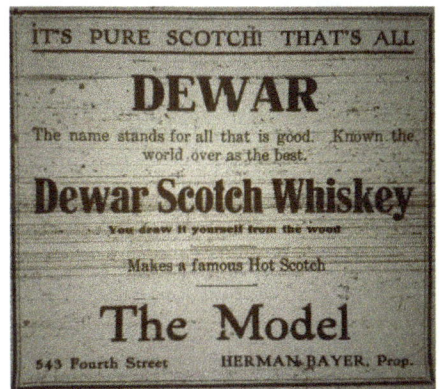

THE MODEL

Size:	Pint
Style:	Coffin
Year:	1900/10
Height:	7½ Inches Tall
Type Top:	Tooled
Color:	Amethyst
Bottom:	1213
Rarity:	Rare

HERMAN BAYER
The Model
543- 4th ST
SANTA ROSA, CAL.

THE MODEL

Size:	Half pint
Style:	Coffin
Year:	1911/16
Height:	6¼ Inches Tall
Type Top:	Tooled
Color:	Clear
Bottom:	1560
Rarity:	Rare

R. R. O'BRIEN
THE MODEL
543 – 4th ST.
SANTA ROSA, CAL.

THE MODEL

Size:	Pint
Style:	Coffin
Year:	1911/16
Height:	6¼ Inches Tall
Type Top:	Tooled
Color:	Clear
Bottom:	1213
Rarity:	Rare

R.R. O'BRIEN
THE MODEL
543 – 4th ST.
SANTA ROSA, CAL.
NET CONTENTS
6 FLUID OZ.

THE MODEL

Paper Label
The Celebrated
Old J. F. Cutter Whisky

R. R. O'Brien Proprietor
Rarity: Rare

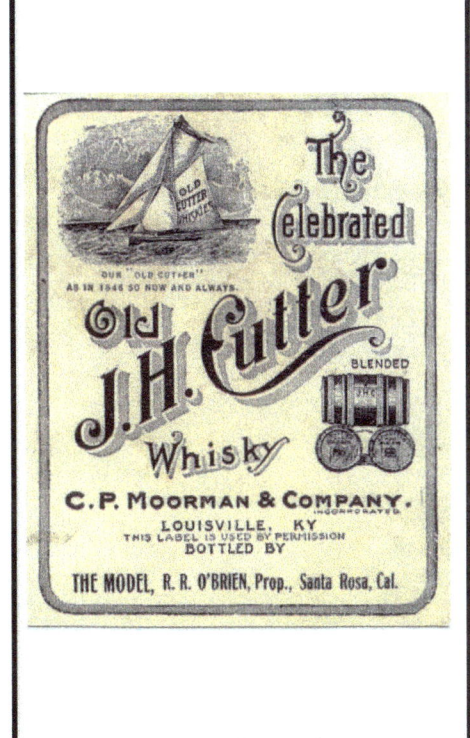

THE MODEL

Size:	24 oz. Fifth
Style:	Cylinder
Year:	1911/16
Height:	11 Inches tall
Type Top:	Tooled
Color:	Amber
Bottom:	#1560
Rarity:	Rare

24 OZ.
THE MODEL
543 4th ST.
SANTA ROSA, CAL.

THE MODEL

Unlisted - The Model - A

Unlisted – Model Saloon - B

K-2 Large 5c

K - 2 Small 5c

K - 111

THE OBERON
440 - Fourth Street
Frank W. Brown & Louis Gnesa
1904 - 1912
Louis Gnesa - 1913 – 1917

Frank W. Brown and Louis Gnesa opened the Oberon Saloon in 1904 at 440 Fourth Street. The 1906 earthquake damaged the Oberon and Brown and Gnesa reopened on the rear of the property on Fifth Street and renamed the business "The Gilt Edge Saloon."

After the Oberon was rebuilt they relocated back into the original location. In 1913, Gnesa purchased Brown's share of the business. The Oberon closed in 1918 because of prohibition. Gnesa's son opened a cigar store at 111 4th Street in 1917.

They also opened an Oberon Saloon in Vallejo after the 1906 earthquake and fire.

Press Democrat, Number 156, May 12, 1901
Louis Gnesa Appears
Louis Gnesa, the local saloon keeper, appeared in Justice Brown's court yesterday morning to answer to the complaint against him by the city marshal charging him with conducting a percentage game, to wit, a nickel in the slot machine, otherwise known as a "money machine." At the time Justice Brown read the complaint to Mr. Gnesa for whom his counsel, J. R. Leppo, Emmet Seawell and VV. F. Cowan, interposed a demurrer. The demurrer urged that the complaint did' not state facts sufficient to constitute a public offense, and further that the complaint does not conform to section's 959, 951 and 952 of the Penal Code. The court overruled the demurrer. A hearing will be given the case tomorrow.

Press Democrat, Number 157, May 14, 1901
Gnesa discharged by Judge Brown Monday
The trial of the case of the State against Louis Gnesa, charged with running a percentage game played for money with money in a slot machine, came off in Justice Brown's court on Monday at 2 o'clock. It occupied just a few minutes. It resulted in the discharge of the defendant. Court Reporter Mrs. Edith Goodman transcribed the testimony. At the outset Assistant District Attorney Berry announced that City Attorney Vaughan would be associated with him. The array of legal talent on the side of the defendant was composed of Attorney J. R. Leppo, Attorney Emmet Seawell and Attorneys Cowan & Julliard.

Upon the inquiry of the Judge, the attorneys said "ready" and off the case went. Charles H. Holmes, city marshal, was called to the witness stand. He was the man who swore out the complaint against Mr. Gnesa. He was asked by Mr. Berry to describe the modus operand! of the slot machine and did so to the best of his ability. The witness explained the charge that it was a "percentage game" by saying that he thought that if it was a game at all it was a percentage game. As to whether it was a percentage game or not the witness testified that he did not know. The machines had been "ordered out" and it became necessary for him to file complaints against those who had them, he said. Judge Brown asked the witness if he could explain whether the

THE OBERON

game was a percentage game or not. Mr. Holmes stated that he could not, but the owners of the machines might be called as witnesses. Mr. Berry announced that Mr. Holmes was the only witness the prosecution had. The defense did not call any witnesses, and the court, after remarking that such evidence as had been adduced could not convict anyone, discharged the defendant.

Press Democrat, Number 14, January 17, 1904
The best of everything
The Oberon a Popular and Well-Appointed Resort.
The Oberon is a well-appointed and popular resort, located at 440 Fourth Street, directly opposite the Occidental Hotel. The proprietors, Frank W. Brown and Louis Gnesa, who conduct their business under the firm name and style of Brown & Gnesa, are both gentlemen who make friends readily and keep them, a fact which, combined with the farther fact that they pay close attention to the wants of their customers at all times, has resulted in building up a fine trade. The bar is supplied with the best of everything, nothing being considered too good for the customers of this house. Card and reading rooms are at the disposition of patrons and few if any details calculated to add to their comfort or convenience are ever overlooked by the management.

Press Democrat, Number 204, August 18, 1905
Arrests made for violating the law
Complaints were sworn out in Justice Atchison's court on Thursday morning charging Louis Gnesa. of the Oberon. Waller Farley and Robert Gainer with disobeying the law prohibiting gambling. The alleged offense was committed on Wednesday night. Assistant District Attorney Thompson was the complaining witness and the proceedings were based on evidence furnished the District Attorney's office by the officers. The cases were called in Justice Atchison's court where the defendants appeared on Thursday afternoon represented by their counsel. Attorney Joe P. Berry, The attorney asked to have the cases continued for two days for the entry of plea by the defendants. The request was granted and the defendants were allowed to go on their own recognizances.

Press Democrat, Number 207, August 22, 1905
Demurrer is interposed
Attorney J. P. Berry has presented a demurrer to the complaint against **Louis Gnesa,** Frank Brown and Walter Farley charging them with gambling and the cases have been continued until Friday afternoon at 2 o'clock to be argued. The demurrers allege insufficiency of the complaint to show an offense. Other grounds are argued.

THE OBERON

Pumpkinseed
Tooled top
4½ Inches tall
Clear glass
Rarity: Extremely Rare

BROWN & GNESA
THE OBERON
SANTA ROSA, CAL.

Pumpkinseed
Tooled top
5½ Inches tall
Clear glass
Rarity: Extremely Rare

BROWN & GNESA
THE OBERON
SANTA ROSA, CAL.

THE OBERON

Coffin Flask
Tooled top
6½ Inches tall
Clear glass
Rarity: Extremely Rare

Line drawing
John Thomas Book

BROWN & GNESA
THE OBERON
SANTA ROSA, CAL.

Picnic flask - Screw top
6¼ inches tall
No Contents on bottom face
Base blank
Rarity: Rare

B & G
OBERON
BROWN & GNESA
SANTA ROSA, CAL.

THE OBERON

Picnic flask - Screw top
6¼ inches tall
No Contents on bottom face
#353 on base
Rarity: Rare

B & G
OBERON
BROWN & GNESA
SANTA ROSA, CAL.

Picnic flask - Screw top
6¼ inches tall
Clear glass
NET CONTENTS 6 OZ.
#998 on base
Rarity: Rare

Note:
LG is Louis Gnesa

LG
OBERON
LOUIS GNESA
SANTA ROSA, CAL.

THE OBERON

Picnic flask - Screw top
7½" inches tall
Clear glass
#2007 on base
Rarity: Rare
Note:
LG is Louis Gnesa

LG
OBERON
LOUIS GNESA
SANTA ROSA, CAL.

After the 1906 earthquake, Brown and Gnesa opened a saloon in Vallejo for a period of less than 6 months while rebuilding the "Gilt Edge" saloon in Santa Rosa.

Picnic flask - Screw top
6¼ inches tall
Clear glass
No Contents on bottom face
#353 on base
Rarity: Rare

B & G
OBERON
BROWN & GNESA
VALLEJO, CAL.

THE RECEPTION

THE RECEPTION
Jap West
431 – 4th ST.

Press Democrat, Number 107, March 17, 1901
To Open "The Reception"

The **Reception saloon,** which is located in the Byington building on Fourth Street, will be re-opened about the middle of next week by Messrs. John Baylor, Jr., and Sid. Tewksbury. The interior has been completely renovated and decorated by Colonel Byington and is one of the finest in the city.

Mr. Baylor is well known in Santa Rosa, having been head driver for Grace Bros. Brewery for the past four years. Mr. Tewksbury is late of Del Monte, San Francisco, and he has very many friends here, where he has been employed at "The Oberon."

The **Reception** will be run as a first class resort, and the young men will no doubt meet with success

Press Democrat, Number 193, 27 June 1901

Mr. Baylor of the **Reception Saloon,** No. 431 Fourth Street, petitioned the council for a retail liquor license for the place. Councilmen Bower, Keegan and Brown were named a committee to consider the application.

K – 80   K – 80 B

THE TAVERN
Al Young
1909 - 1915
Press Democrat, Number 184, 8 August 1909

WANTED —A woman to do housekeeping and cook for one, and generally useful in small road house. Apply A. **Young,** The **Tavern,** Healdsburg road, 1 mile from town

Unlisted

THE WELCOME SALOON

A. Casselli Proprietor 1901 - 1904

Press Democrat, Number 52, December 12, 1901
Chop House Department
Something new. Chop House Department. Meals on short order from 10c up. Call and see us. The **Welcome Saloon,** 123 Fourth Street..

Press Democrat, Number 29, 4 February 1904
ANGRY HUSBAND SENDS A BULLET AT HIS WIFE A DOUBLE TRAGEDY WAS NARROWLY AVERTED
Considerable excitement on
LOWER SECOND STREET AT NINE O'CLOCK YESTERDAY EVENING
Statements Made By the Gun Wielder and His Wife Show Bad State of Affairs
She Says He Was Victim of Unwarranted Jealousy But He Says Nay

Shortly before nine o'clock Wednesday night the report of a pistol, followed a moment later by a woman's screams and the cries of children, aroused the neighborhood of lower Second street and in a remarkably short time there was all kinds of excitement. The gun wielder was A. Casselli, proprietor of The **Welcome saloon** on lower Fourth Street, and his wife's body furnished the mark for his bullet. Fortunately, however, the ball embedded itself in the wall of the room in which the affray took place, missing the woman by the closest kind of a margin. At the time of the shooting the man behind the gun stood on the threshold of the living room in the little house opposite the Santa Rosa Tanning Company's tannery. In the room were Mrs. Casselli and her five children. Unwarranted jealousy on the part of the husband is the cause assigned by the wife.

The husband claims that he had sufficient grounds for being jealous. And there you are. Immediately after the shooting a hurried telephone message was sent to police headquarters and as quickly as possible Police Officers J. M. Boyes, 1. N. Lindley and Don McIntosh were at the scene. They found the woman in a very excited condition and this was excusable after the remarkably close escape from death she had experienced at the hands of her husband. The little children were also in a state of fear. After learning the details Policemen Boyes and Lindley started out to arrest Casselli, Policeman McIntosh remaining on guard at the residence, as the woman feared that her husband might return and renew the attack. Policemen Boyes and Lindley arrested Casselli outside his **saloon.** He was searched but had no pistol on him at the time, having previously left it in the **saloon.** He took the officers inside and back of the bar the weapon was lying where he had dropped it after taking out, the four remaining cartridges and the empty one. He was also excited but went along with the officers to the police station very quietly. The man, the officers say, has the reputation of being a quiet respectable fellow.

He was assigned to a cell at the city's hostelry on Hinton Avenue. It seems that when Casselli fired the shot at his wife, he says that he was so excited at the time he did not know what he was doing. He was standing only a few feet away from her. The room is a small one anyway and considerable space is taken up with a stove and other furniture. Consequently it is a wonder that he missed striking her when this is taken into consideration and the added fact that she is a stout

THE WELCOME SALOON

woman, hardly of the average height. A reporter visited the place a short time after the excitement and had a talk with Mrs. Casselli and was shown the place where the bullet was

Imbedded in the wall. Mrs. Casselli, when asked what prompted her husband to take her life, stated that she did not know and suggested that he had suddenly lost control of his mental faculties. She said that she heard footsteps on the porch and that the door had opened suddenly and her husband pointed a pistol at her and fired. The shot extinguished the lamp burning in the room and had left everything in darkness. She left the room as hurriedly as possible after she had recovered from the temporary shock and had ascertained that she had not been struck by the bullet. "I got under the table," put in one of the curly headed girls, who during the interview sat with her head resting on her hands on the table. Mrs. Casselli was asked whether there was any ground for her husband to be jealous of her and whether she knew of any reason why he should attempt her life and she replied that she knew of no reason. To others she admitted that some man had said that he loved her and of course she was not responsible for such an expression of sentiment on his part.

The man in question was a bartender who had assisted her husband in the **saloon,** Baccherini by name, who had been taking his meals at the house. According to Casselli this man Baccherini is the cause of all the trouble, during the time when he, Casselli, was befriending him. The stories of the husband and wife differ on this point. When seen at the police station at half past ten o'clock Casselli was asked for his version of the shooting. He told his pan in a plain, unhesitating manner. He admitted that he fired the shot and at the time he was in a state of mind that he did not know what he was doing. He stated that he had been suspicious of Boccherini's actions towards Mrs. Casselli for some time and on Monday he said he confirmed his suspicions that everything was not as it should be. He did not go home after Monday, he said, in consequence of what he had learned. Casselli told his interviewer that early Wednesday evening Baccherini came to the **saloon** and asked him (Casselli) why he was mad at him and urged him to take a drink and shake hands. Casselli said that he told Baccherini that he had good reason to be mad at him.

Finally, acting upon the advice of others in the **saloon,** Casselli took a drink with Baccherini and the rest. Soon after this, Casselli stated to the reporter and the officers, Baccherini told him that his suspicions regarding his (Boccherini's) conduct towards Mrs. Casselli were true. After this, Casselli maintains, Baccherini repeated his assertions in the presence of other men in the **saloon.** After some more talk Casselli said that Baccherini went away and a short time afterwards he was informed by a friend that Baccherini had gone to the Casselli residence. Casselli then made up his mind to investigate and went to the outside of the house and overheard a conversation going on inside between the man and woman.

He says that he heard Mrs. Casselli upbraid Baccherini for having told her husband anything and Baccherini replied in this way: "I would die for you." Then, he said, he heard something about getting rid of the children. When he heard the conversation about the children, who he professes to love very dearly, Casselli says his blood boiled and he became so excited that if he had had a pistol with him he would have undoubtedly used it. He then went up town and a friend got some

THE WELCOME SALOON

cartridges for him and he went back to the house. He soon ascertained that Baccherini had left. He heard his wife talking to one of the children and then losing all control of himself he stepped to the door and fired into the room. After the shot he struck a match to see if the bullet had struck any of the occupants of the room and seeing that it had not he left. In response to a request sent by his wife, Casselli sent some money from the jail to buy food for the children. The man's story was a long one and it was easy to gather from his relating of the details that he had been a very suspicious and probably jealous man. He even went so far as to say that if he had had a weapon on a previous occasion there would probably have been a double tragedy.

Mrs. Casselli also has friends here who have classed her as a respectable woman. She denies the statements made by her husband and reiterates that he was insanely Jealous and that was all the matter. She stated that she and her husband have had a little trouble before but nothing like what occurred on Wednesday night. She seems very fond of her children. The crowd of people attracted to the Casselli residence after the shooting was so great that Policeman Boyes had to disperse it and permitted no one to enter the house outside of Mrs. Caselli's relatives. At the jail Casselli was visited by a number of his friends. Baccherini was one of the callers, and the man in the cell became so enraged that he tried to reach him through the bars and there would probably have been something doing if he had.

Press Democrat, Number 263, 5 November 1904
Despite the fact that the announcement has been, published repeatedly numerous times daily inquiries come to the office of County Tax Collector Frank Grace asking when "taxes became delinquent." The first Installment of state and county taxes become delinquent after the last Monday in November, on November 28. Under an attachment issued out of the Superior Court Sheriff Grace has levied an execution upon the **"Welcome Saloon"** on Fourth Street, the property of A. Caselli. Caselli is the man who spent ten days in Jail recently for failure to pay his wife the amount of alimony ordered by the court. He took the pauper's oath and was released from custody.

Unlisted

THE WHEN
(AKA the Recall)

O. C. McPROUD Proprietor - 1912 - 1916
A. W. Tickner Proprietor 1916 - 1918
408 Fourth Street

Press Democrat, Number 295, 18 December 1912
Action Taken at the Meeting Held Here Last Night by the City Fathers

The City Council at its regular mid-month meeting last night granted renewals of thirty-four liquor licenses, and refused renewal to three on the report of the special committee to whom the applications were referred two weeks ago. The licenses renewed and their location are as follows: L. **O.** Battaglia, 609 Adams street; Paul Pascio and Luigi Riggl, 23 West Sixth street; Theo. Ferranl, 117 Fourth street; Garrett M. Kidd, 412 Fourth street; R. R. O'Brien, 643 Fourth Street; Guidotti Bros., 621 Adams street: Hadrich & Co., 436 Fourth street; Walter Schmid, 421 Fourth; E. U. Bernard!, Fifth and A; **O. C. McProud, 408 Fourth;** Jones & Matthews, 531 Fourth; Louis Gnesa, 436 Fourth; Thos. Gemetti, 576 Third; Geo. Stocking, 314 Fourth; Bane Bros., 439 Fourth; Cavagna & Finaci, 201 Fourth; J. Meraldi, 1 West Sixth; Loporl & Tomasoli, 8 Fourth; Girolo & Perotto, 123 Fourth; Bettini & Arlgoni, Fourth and Wilson;, J. W. Wood, First and Main; J. **C.** Sarraihi, 103 Main; **C.** G. Christian, 236 Fourth; M. Albera, 301 Fourth; Karl Schmlt, 105 Fourth; B. Bettini, Fifth and Wilson; M. A. Davis, 207 B Street; Edward Ahvenn, 319 Fourth; D. Quinlan, 636 Third; Beswick & Gardiner, 845 Fourth; P. H. Quinn, Overton Hotel; Dan Picken, Dougherty-Shea Building, Mendocino Street; Wright & Wilson, Second and Main; Brittain & Brunk, 646 Third.

Press Democrat, Number 87, April 9, 1916
SALOON CHANGES HANDS
A. W. Tickner of Portland has taken up his residence in Santa Rosa and purchased the "The When" saloon. The name of the place has been changed to the "Recall Saloon".

K -106

THE WINDSOR

637 – Fourth Street (Hahman Building)
W. B. Sanborn – Proprietor – 1885

Press Democrat, Number 181, 12 February 1889
Billiard Hall Thief.

A few weeks ago a $30 set of billiard balls was stolen from **W. B. Sanborn's** saloon. The set was replaced with a new one when all hope of finding the thief had been given up. The new set was broken Sunday by the theft of another ball, the thief this time being satisfied to take one at a time. Mr. **Sanborn** regards the last theft as a reproach of his carelessness, and the balls will be kept under lock and key.

Unlisted

THE WRENN

WILBER C. WRENN
301 Fourth Street 1914 – 1918

K - 108

Unlisted

TOSCANO HOTEL

F. Guidotti
7th & Adams Street

Press Democrat, Number 90, 16 April 1904

FIRE DAMAGES THE TOSCANO HOTEL CONFLAGRATION ORIGINATED IN ROOM IN THE UPPER STORY OF THE BUILDING
Exact Cause of the Fire Not Known
Building Drenched With Copious Supply of Water Thrown

Considerable damage was done by a flue fire at the Toscano hotel at Seventh and Adams streets yesterday evening about half past five o'clock, for which the fire department was called by an alarm rung in from Box 25.

The fire started in room 3 on the upper story of the hotel building. The room was gutted and its contents were destroyed. In addition other pails of the building were charred, but owing to the prompt work of the department the damage was not nearly as serious as he otherwise would have been, as the flames had considerable headway at the time of the alarm and it seemed as if the entire upper portion of the place was on fire.

The smoke was so dense that the firemen had considerable difficulty in at first locating the seat of the conflagration. The room in which the fire started was like a blazing when the department arrived and the fire was spreading. Two streams of water were quickly poured on the flames and the fire was soon extinguished. The building was drenched with water and this and the smoke will necessitate the complete renovation of a part of the interior of the building.

Many willing hands removed most of the furniture and effects from the building and these articles were piled up here and there, some distance from the scene of the conflagration. The hotel is owned and occupied by Mrs. T. Guidotti. The fire was discovered by A. Guidotti. The origin of the fire at present is somewhat of a mystery. There was no stove in the room and the flue from the stove below runs up in another room.

The fire seemed to have started in the corner of the apartment. The occupants of the hotel could not account for the fire, and there were suggestions that the origin might have been of an incendiary natural when Adams picked up a piece of newspaper in the room most damaged by the fire and it smelt strongly of coal oil. Strange enough this piece of paper was not singed and everything else in the room was charred. Another report at the fire was that a man had laid his lighted pipe on the bed in the room, hut this story was not confirmed. A defective flue was also suggested. The building was insured.

The water was played on the flames with so much effect that the roof overhead was not damaged. The fire occasioned some excitement among those living in the immediate neighborhood of the hotel and some of them were prepared to remove their belongings and did do so until assured that the danger of the fire spreading was past.

TOSCANO HOTEL

Press Democrat, Number 124, May 20, 1910
Violated the Ordinance

Police Officer I. N. Lindley filed a complaint Thursday in the City Recorder's Court against Guidotti Bros., proprietors of the Toscano hotel bar, for a violation of the midnight closing ordinance. It was claimed that the bar was kept open and liquor served to the circus employees after hours. An appearance was made during the afternoon by one of the brothers engaged in the business and a plea of guilty entered. Recorder Bagley assessed a fine of $20 which was paid promptly.

K – 101 – Small 5c   **Unlisted - Large 5c**

WESTERN HOTEL

2 – 4 Fourth Street
(Opposite Railroad Depot)

WESTERN HOTEL
1906 Earthquake Damage
Sonoma County Library Photo

WESTERN HOTEL
After the Earthquake
Sonoma County Library Photo

The Western Hotel was originally a two-story wood framed building opened in 1878 owned by M. Byrnes with 31 rooms and no bathrooms. Rooms were priced at .25 cents and .50 cents per night.

The Western Hotel was the busiest hotel in the city when it changed hands in the late 1880's. It was situated next to the train tracks (known as Tar Flats) and because of its location the first choice for tourists. At the time, Santa Rosa was the connection for travelers on their way to the Russian River and the Geysers.

On July 4, 1896, Michael McNamara, purchased the Western Hotel. The hotel became more of a boarding house at this time and the laborers who stayed there had to go to a barber shop once a week to bathe in the public baths for .25 cents.

At the turn of the century, the area became known as one of the roughest areas in the city. The Western became a hangout for the tougher elements in town but the tourist continued to stay at the hotel because of its location.

On July 4, 1902, six years to the day that McNamara purchased the hotel, a fire swept through the neighborhood destroying the hotel and the original wooden train station. The wooden structure was again destroyed by fire the hotel was rebuilt by stonemason's Peter Maroni, Angelo Sodini, Natale Forni and Massimo Galeazzi.

In 1903, John Doda, purchased the property and built a stone two-story hotel. He leased it to John Fumasoli and Antone Lepori. Again the hotel was a thriving business located next to the train tracks. Whiskey was selling for .10 cents a drink in the northwest corner bar.

The 1906 earthquake caused an exterior wall to collapse injuring several persons and killing Joseph Domeniconi, who was an employee. It was the only hotel left partially standing in Santa Rosa after the quake.

McNamara sold to a Mr. Doda who then sold to Henry P. Reynaud of Petaluma in 1917. Reynaud owned the building for only two years. He sold to Peter and Mary Carzanzi and Peter Tenti. Carzanzi and Tenti owned the building until 1945 and sold to Thomas and Norman Alexander.

One of the hotel regulars, Terry Fitts, was one of the three men lynched at Franklin Cemetery for killing the local sheriff.

WESTERN HOTEL

Size: Half Pint
Style: Pumpkinseed
Year: 1900
Height: 5¼ Inches Tall
Type Top: Tooled
Color: Clear
Bottom: Blank
Rarity: Extremely Rare

**WESTERN HOTEL
SANTA ROSA
NET CONTENTS 5 OZ.**

WESTERN HOTEL

Size: Pint
Style: Pumpkinseed
Year: 1900
Height: 6¾ Inches Tall
Type Top: Tooled
Color: Clear
Bottom: Blank
Rarity: Extremely Rare

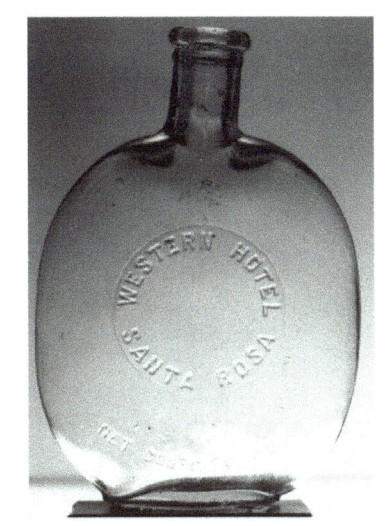

**WESTERN HOTEL
SANTA ROSA
NET CONTENTS 10 OZ.**

WESTERN HOTEL

Size: Half Pint
Style: Coffin
Year: 1900
Height: 6¼ Inches Tall
Type Top: Tooled
Color: Clear
Bottom: Blank
Rarity: Rare

**WESTERN HOTEL
SANTA ROSA
NET CONTENTS
5 OZ.**

WESTERN HOTEL

Size: Half Pint
Style: Coffin
Year: 1900
Height: 6½ Inches Tall
Type Top: Tooled
Color: Clear
Bottom: Blank
Rarity: Rare

**WESTERN HOTEL
SANTA ROSA
NET CONTENTS
6 OZ.**

K - 102 - Large 5c

K – 103 – Small 5c

K - 104

K-105

CLOVERDALE

FRANK SPENCER SALOON

Corner of Eastside West
Frank Spencer started his career at the U. S. Hotel in Cloverdale in 1878 as a steward. He joined John Dixon in 1883 and opened the Dixon & Spencer saloon. Spencer's brother, John tended bar for them. Frank Spencer became the sole owner approximately 1887.

Size:	**Pint**
Style:	**Pumpkinseed**
Year:	**1900**
Height:	**6½ Inches tall**
Type Top:	**Tooled**
Color:	**Clear**
Bottom:	
Rarity:	**Extremely Rare**

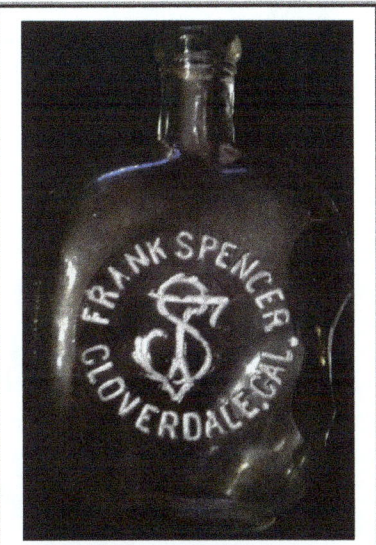

FRANK SPENCER
F S (Monogram)
CLOVERDALE, CAL.

K - 21

CLOVERDALE
U – AUTO BAR
Mitchell Bros.

K – 15   K - 16

K – 4   Unlisted

U. S. HOTEL

Unlisted

CLOVERDALE

GIBSON

K - 5

PALACE SALOON

Mirror Face:
GOOD FOR 10c IN TRADE THE PALACE, CLOVERDALE, CAL.
Evelyn Nesbitt in photo

ADDITIONAL HEALDSBURG BOTTLES

HEALDSBURG

Year: 1915
Height: 10½ Inches tall
Type Top: Tooled
Color: Amber
Bottom: 55C

**WINE CREEK
VINEYARDS
SELECT VINTAGE
HEALDSBURG
SONOMA, CO.
CALIF.**

K – 35

HEALDSBURG

OWL HOLLOW WHISKEY
MASSONI & FAVA

Style:	Half pint pumpkinseed
Year:	1908
Height:	5¾ Inches tall
Type Top:	Tooled top with cork
Color:	Clear with paper label
Bottom:	V
Rarity:	Rare

OWL HOLLOW WHISKEY MASSONI & FAVA HEALDSBURG, CAL. THOROUGHLY MATURED

OWL HOLLOW WHISKEY
MASSONI & FAVA

Style:	Pint pumpkinseed
Year:	1908
Height:	6¾ Inches tall
Type Top:	Tooled top with cork
Color:	Clear with paper label
Bottom	*
Rarity:	Rare

OWL HOLLOW WHISKEY MASSONI & FAVA HEALDSBURG, CAL. THOROUGHLY MATURED

PETALUMA WHISKEY BOTTLES

KELLER'S BAR

Press Democrat, Number 225, 20 September 1913
Pay Fine of $160.00
Fred Keller, a Petaluma saloon man, paid a fine of $160.00 on Wednesday for selling liquor to a woman there. A second offense, the Courier says, will mean a forfeiture of his license.

Pint Dandy Screw Top Flask

KELLER'S BAR
PETALUMA

Rick Siri Bottle

PETALUMA WHISKEY BOTTLES

P. MORVILLE'S
AAA
OLD BOURBON
1864

Quart Bottle

SEBASTOPOL

SPEAS MANUFACTURING & DISTILLERY PLANT
Corner Petaluma Avenue & McKinley Streets
Speas Plant from 1934 to 1990

Vinegar & Apple Brandy

Healdsburg Tribune, Enterprise and Scimitar, Number 36, 14 June 1934
APPLE BRANDY PLANT TO OPEN AT SEBASTOPOL
An apple brandy distillery, believed to be the first to enter large scale production in the west since repeal, has been established here and will be ready for operation by June 15, it was announced by officials of the plant Thursday. The distillery, located in a four story reinforced concrete bonded warehouse, will have an 8000 barrel capacity. The plant will be operated by the Speas Manufacturing Company, with executive offices in Kansas City, Mo., and plants throughout the country. The Speas Company has operated a plant at Sebastopol for several years for the production of fruit pectin, vinegars and other by-products, and has remodeled its warehouse to accommodate the new brandy distillery. The firm already has been granted the necessary authority by the federal alcohol control administration to proceed with the apple brandy production program. V. K. Speas is the company's president, and F. M. Butler is the manager of the Pacific coast division.

SEBASTOPOL

Madera Tribune, Number 94, 31 August 1955
Warehouse Blaze at Sebastopol Is Investigated
A fire of undetermined origin destroyed a huge apple storage warehouse here early today, ruining an estimated $240,000 worth of apples. The fire broke out about midnight and razed the **Sebastopol** Apple Growers Union warehouse No. 1 in the center of town. The warehouse was owned by a grower's cooperative. 1 The building was packed to the roof with boxes of dried apples, in which had not been moved due to a strike of the AFL Teamsters Union against eight canneries in the area. High Flames As the fire spread through the 250-foot long building it shot flames 300 feet into the air burning 500 tons of dried apples owned by the Analy Marketing Cooperative Association. The flames also damaged the rear of the **Speas** apple brandy distillery next door. The fire was brought under control within an hour. Nine fire trucks, including units from **Sebastopol,** Santa Rosa, Graton and the Forest Service, battled the blaze. Fire department officials here announced that they would begin an immediate investigation.

SPEAS APPLE JACK BRANDY
Half Pint
Rarity: **Rare**

SEBASTOPOL

SPEAS APPLE BRANDY
FIFTH
Rarity: Rare

SEBASTOPOL

BIG WINERY DEAL
Italian Swiss Colony Buys the Sebastopol Winery

Controls a Big Part of the Wine Business in Sonoma County at the Present Time
The Italian-Swiss colony has added another large Sonoma county winery to the number it owns and operates. The colony has acquired the Martin Feusler, also known as the Juilliard winery at **Sebastopol.** Several days ago it was rumored that the colony were casting about to obtain possession of the winery at **Sebastopol** and on Saturday morning a Press Democrat representative interviewed P. C. Rossi, president of the colony, at the California Northwestern depot and he confirmed the rumor and stated that the formal transfer of the property would be made in a few days The colony in addition to its vast interests at Asti in this county, has also acquired possession of the Cloverdale winery, the Fulton' winery and the **Sebastopol** winery. It will formally take possession of the Cloverdale winery at the time of .the annual meeting of the Cloverdale wine company in June. At present John Cooley is efficiently managing the business.

SANTA ROSA

I DeTURK SANTA ROSA
LACHMAN & JACOBI PETALUMA
ASTI SEBASTOPOL
Private collection of John C. Burton

Isaac DeTurk, an early pioneer in the California wine industry arrived in Sonoma County in 1858. The son of an Indiana viticulturist, DeTurk established Belle Mount Vineyards at the foot of Bennett Peak in 1862, and founded another vineyard in Cloverdale in 1863. His first crop was sold to Barney Hoen. The second vineyard, he processed himself to produce the first DeTurk Winery

Sometime between 1870-1874 DeTurk bought a burned out winery located between Railroad and Adams streets in Santa Rosa to house his Santa Rosa Winery, also known as DeTurk Winery

The 2-storied brick buildings included: a cellar containing 84 tanks, each holding 2,000 gallons for a total capacity of 300,000 gallons; a crushing room holding 30 tanks, each with 2,000 gallon capacity, for a total of 66,000 gallons, and two crushers with a combined volume of 6 tons an hour; with a complete brandy distillery capable of manufacturing 10,000 gallons a day.

**Copy of a stone litho advertisement. Approximately 1895.
Original in John C. Burton collection
Has been reprinted as poster and postcard by Nanci L. Burton**

I. DeTURK

1890/1895

Fifth
Clear cylinder
11 Inches tall
Sloping shoulders

I. DE TURK
*** (Three stars)
NET CONTENTS 1/5 GAL.

John Louder Bottle

1890/1895

Fifth
Clear cylinder
11½ Inches tall
Straight neck

I. DE TURK in banner
TRADE (Monogram) MARK
VINEYARD
SANTA ROSA, CAL.

1895/1905

Fifth
Amber cylinder
11 Inches tall
Brandy top
Brandy neck
402 H on base

I. DE. TURK (Arched)
TRADE CMM MARK
C. M. MANN
SUCCESSORS
SAN FRANCISCO
CAL.

1905/1917

Fifth
Amber cylinder
10¾ Inches tall
Brandy top
Brandy neck

I. DE TURK (Arched)
TRADE (W H & Co) MARK
Wm. HOELSCHER & CO.
SUCCESSORS
SAN FRANCISCO
CAL.

1905/1917

Fifth
Amber cylinder
10¾ Inches tall
Brandy top
Brandy neck

**I. DE TURK (Arched)
TRADE (W H & Co) MARK
Wm. HOELSCHER & CO.**

**SUCCESSORS
SAN FRANCISCO
CAL.
NET CONTENTS
1 PINT AND 9 – OZ.**

1918/1919

Fifth
Amber cylinder
10½ Inches tall
Screw top
Brandy neck

I. De Turk (Arched script)
(W H Co)
*Wm. HOELSCHER & CO.
SAN FRANCISCO* (Script)

According to the 1937 edition of *History of Sonoma County* by Ernest Finley, Joseph T. Grace, one of the four Grace Brothers involved with the Grace Brothers Brewery was the sole proprietor of the winery, at least for that year.

Cardboard barrel-end from Grace Bros. Inc. (Joseph T. Grace)

Pint Muscat twist-top wine bottle. Grace Bros. Inc. (Joseph T. Grace)

1918/1919

**I. De TURK
DRY SAUTERNE
Wm. HOELSCHER & Co**

**Fifth
Clear cylinder
11¾ Inches tall
14& by-volume
Cork closure**

**I De TURK PEN KNIFE
Wm. HOELSCHER & Co
San Francisco, Cal.**

SANTA ROSA

KOPF & DONOVAN
3rd & Wilson Streets
C. Louis Koph
Ney Donovan

SANTA ROSA

KOPF & DONOVAN
3rd & Wilson Streets
C. Louis Koph
Ney Donovan

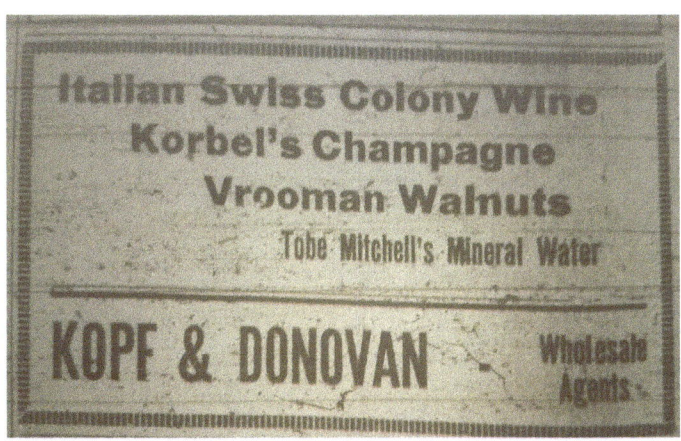

SANTA ROSA

HAYES & KOPF
3rd & Wilson Streets
Hayes
C. Louis Koph

PETALUMA

LACHMAN & JACOBI

By Ed Mannion

Fame is fleeting, to coin a phrase, and never was this truer than the now almost forgotten Lachman & Jacobi Winery of Petaluma and outlying localities such as San Francisco and New York City. At one time the firm was the largest manufacturing institution north of the bay.
It seems rather strange the company's name, nearly 100 years old, isn't known among California collectors. Even the bottles are scarce. The writer has seen only five examples of such glassware and he has four of them. Of course much of the stock was shipped back east in tank cars and paper labels on the bottles have made collecting difficult locally.

Lachman & Jacobi produced wines and brandies. Its South San Francisco plant was destroyed in the earthquake and fire of 1906 and soon after (less than a month in fact) the old Shirley property on the northwest corner of Washington & Hopper Streets in Petaluma was purchased out from under the nose the California Northwestern Railway, which had been dickering for the land. Within five days ground was broken for the first of a network of buildings. By October the local press reported work on more storage facilities was progressing and "the company is receiving much wine and is shipping great quantities."

Incidentally, several newspaper stories in later years recalling the 1906 catastrophe, said water was shipped to San Francisco from Petaluma on the steamer "Gold", using wine casks from the winery. This would have been trick as the plant was smoldering in South San Francisco at the time.

Originally the complex covered 10 acres of land, later reduced to 7½ acres, and had a storage capacity of over 5,000,000 gallons of wine and 500,000 gallons brandy. Eight separate buildings were involved with the largest covering an area of 400 by 150 feet. Other structures included the United States Bonded Warehouse, the aging and bottling cellars, shipping building, Sherry House, Cooper Shop, Boiler House and the cement tank building consisting of 18 reinforced, glass lined cement tanks with an average capacity of 30,500 gallons each. The main building contained a number of 60,000 gallon wooden tanks. Hugh lawns and flower gardens were placed between and around the various structures.

Lachman & Jacobi dated (not each other) from 1876 and was for years engaged in purchasing wines and brandies and getting them ready for Market by aging, blending and so forth. The firm started raising its own grapes and manufacturing wine, necessitating a large concentration plant for the various processes. This is what was built in Petaluma. Lachman & Jacobi's export trade was worldwide wherever wine was consumed.

In 1915, officers were J. J. Jacobi, president; A. L. Jacobi, Vice-president and treasurer; W. Sommer, secretary; and Colonel E. S. Ciprico in charge of the Petaluma establishment. At this time the San Francisco office was located at Pine and Battery Streets. Warehouses were maintained in Fresno, San Francisco, and Lodi as well as in New York City, New Orleans, Chicago and St. Louis.

Prohibition put the gun to the head of Lachman & Jacobi and the Volstead Act of October 1919 pulled the trigger. For months the complex remained empty.

The Petaluma Argus announced a 1922 Christmas present to the city when National Ice and Storage Company of California purchased from the California Wine Association, all "the monster plant of Lachman & Jacobi excepting the building purchased by the Poultry Producers." The story pointed out that two spurs of the Northwestern Pacific traversed the grounds, and tracks of the Petaluma & Santa Rosa Electric Railway were nearby; also that the site was close to the steamer landing. The winery had made good use of all the transportation advantages.

SPIRITS BOTTLES OF THE OLD WEST by Bill & Betty Wilson has a photograph of a Lachman & Jacobi bottle on page 94. Descriptive matter on the bottle does not mention Petaluma and neither does the embossing on the bottle, showing only the names of San Francisco and New York. The writer has the same bottle with a label on the other side reading:

Especially Selected for the Bottle Collector

CALIFORNIA
OLD SUPERIOR
PORT

ESTABLISHED 1876 (monogram) ESTABLISHED 1876
Lachman & Jacobi
SAN FRANCISCO   NEW YORK
PETALUMA, CAL.

Although the winery has its name listed in area directories after 1906, officials evidently did not believe in purchasing advertising space. An exception was Anna Morrison Reed's monthly publication called *The Northern Crown*, printed first in Ukiah and then in Petaluma. No doubt Anna was put into budget because as early as 1916 she was running articles entitled "Prohibition Is Piracy"; "Why True Californians Dislike Prohibition"; "Why Germany Sends Beer To The Front"; and wrote editorials with thoughts as "Is it not strange that wet England produced a Shakespeare, wet Germany a Schiller, a Bismarck, wet America, a Jefferson, a Washington and a Lincoln, while Prohibition Turkey never produced a single great man in all centuries since Mohammed?

An ad in the *Crown* magazine mentioned the Lachman & Jacobi product was the wine deluxe of European connoisseurs and also could be obtained at any of the leading wine establishments of Petaluma. Another advertisement showed a bottle of sherry with the name "Invalid" on the label.

The address of the Lachman & Jacobi location is 325 East Washington Street, north across Washington from the railroad depot. Two fires wiped out a portion of the complex extending along the railroad track. What remains of the old winery was sold last year by the United States Cold Storage Company to the Kiechnefer Company, developer of the proposed Golden Eagle Shopping Center along East Washington on the east side of the river. New owners have said they are contemplating turning the 45,000 square-foot building into a center along the lines of Ghirardelli Square and the Cannery in San Francisco. The location may see some more bottles again.

Thank you Ed you are missed and we always enjoyed your presence and wisdom…………………..JB

SANTA ROSA CIGAR TOKENS

I. W. BERNSTEIN'S

- Isaac W Bernstein--Born May 1874--Died April 1955
- 1897 Press Democrat article mentions IW Bernstein cigars
- 1901 SF Call article, busted for slot machines along with Louis Gnesa
- 1903 directory gives address as 535 4th St./Occidental Hotel
- 1905 directory address is St Rose Hotel
- 1908 and later he is listed as insurance agent in Alameda, SF, Oakland, and then San Jose.

> SANTA ROSA, May 10.—City Marshal Holmes to-day swore out a warrant against I. W. Bernstein and Louis Gnesa, the former a cigar dealer and the latter one of the proprietors of the Oberon saloon, charging them with maintaining slot machines contrary to law. The law will be tested.

K – 4

K - 5

KURLANDER'S

St. Helena

Press Democrat, Number 214, 14 September 1909
SID KURLANDER ALMOST LOSES CIGAR STORE
Sid Kurlander's cigar store narrowly escaped destruction by fire In St. Helena on Sunday morning. All His stock was moved In the nick of time. The fire started in a restaurant adjoining his place of business. Fortunately the fire was checked before it boned the **Kurlander** establishment.

Press Democrat, Number 297, 13 October 1910
Sidney Kurlander Here
Sidney Kurlander, who has been in the cigar business in St. Helena for a number of years, has sold out his place and has returned with his family to live in this city. He has not yet decided upon his future plans.

K - 52

LA BRAZORIA

BOWER & MERCIER CIGAR STORE

K - 9

K - 10

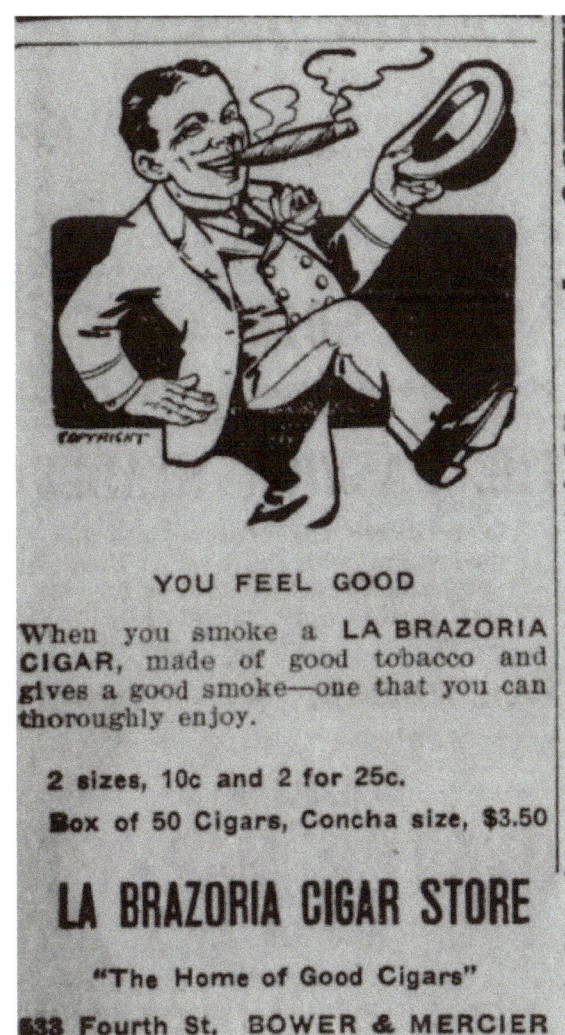

YOU FEEL GOOD

When you smoke a LA BRAZORIA CIGAR, made of good tobacco and gives a good smoke—one that you can thoroughly enjoy.

2 sizes, 10c and 2 for 25c.

Box of 50 Cigars, Concha size, $3.50

LA BRAZORIA CIGAR STORE

"The Home of Good Cigars"

633 Fourth St.   BOWER & MERCIER

MAC KILLOP BROS.

Press Democrat, Number 296, December 19, 1912

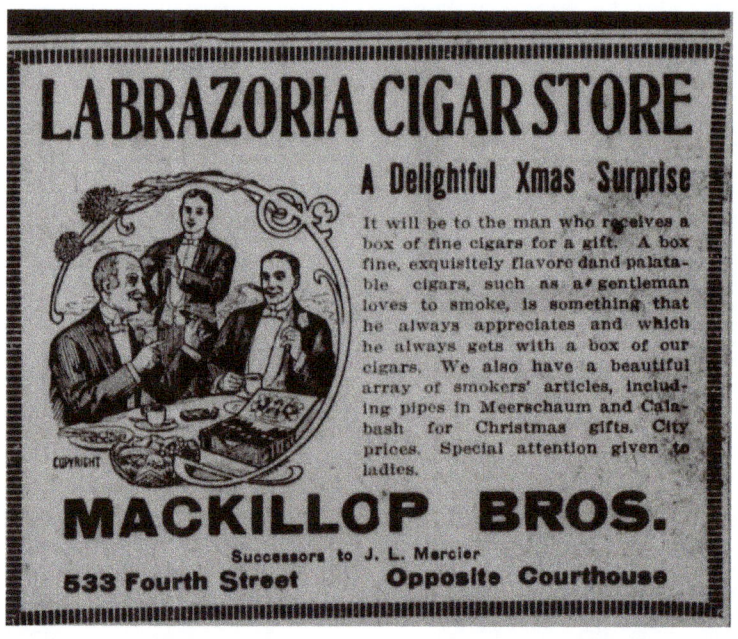

K – 62

K – 63

Unlisted

MUTHER

- Frank Muther Sr. Born 1848, died Dec. 3, 1927
- Frank Muther Jr. Born Jan 14, 1874, died Oct 21, 1947
- Muther is 1880 cigar maker
- Frank Sr. was also Santa Rosa's first paid fire chief from 1894 - April 1912
- Jan 1, 1906 at which time the name was changed to Muther & Son Cigars until Senior's death in 1927
- Frank Jr. is listed in 1910, 20, and 30 as Tobacconist.
- 1940 he is listed as a night watchman.
- Both are buried in SR Odd Fellows Cemetery, Plot 21

K- 67

K – 67 A

Unlisted

INDIAN CIGAR STORE

Muther's sign of the big Indian

K – 46   K - 47

RAMSEY CIGAR STORE

Henry T Ramsey

- 1903   Listed in Santa Rosa, 20 Main Street occupation poultry
- 1908-1910 listed with no occupation.
- 1911 listed as deputy sheriff.
- 1913 no listing.
- 1915 Cigars 301 4th St.

K – 79 – B

K - 79

WALTER SCHMID CIGAR STORE
231 – 4th Street
(Inside Germania)

- 1899 and 1903 proprietor, Germania Hotel 105-7-9 4th Street
- 1905, 08, 10, 11 Schmid & Ritter Saloon 415 4th Street
- 1913, 15 Schmid Liquors 421 4th Street
- 1924 Prindle & Schmid Cigars 225 4th Street
- (Prindle former partner with J. M. Roney)
- 1926, 30 Schmid Cigars 225 4th Street

Unlisted

GEORGE W. WELLS

- 1903 farmer, 203 West 8th Street
- 1905 cigars, 303 Mendocino Avenue
- 1908 real estate, 203 W. 8th Street
- 1910, 11, 13, 15 real estate, 133 4th Street, Sebastopol

January 5, 1904

> Miles H. Peerman has sold out his cigar stand at Fourth and Mendocino streets to George Wells.

March 13, 1907

> George Wells has sold out the stock in his cigar store to Bowers & Mercier and has retired from the business on account of poor health. Mr. Wells' friends all hope he will soon feel strong and well again.

Unlisted

THE PAST TIME

T. J. Gibson
509 Fourth Street

September 1889

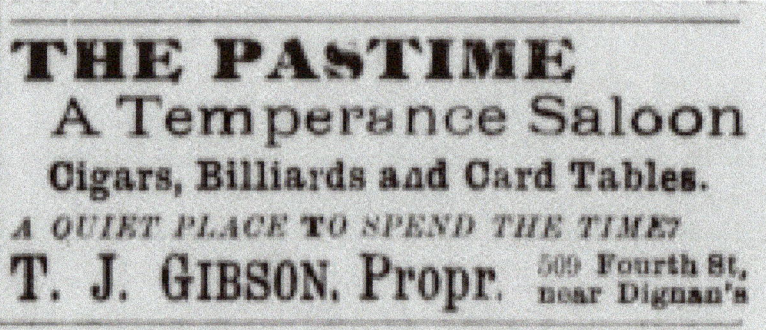

K – 77

www.ingramcontent.com/pod-product-compliance
Lightning Source LLC
Chambersburg PA
CBHW061137010526
44107CB00069B/2968

ACKNOWLEDGEMENTS

For encouragement over the years, for the many discussions and debates, the liberal correspondence, and the sharing of information and material, I gratefully acknowledge the following: My old friend, the late Milt Deno; Gene Smith and Dale Delaruelle of Harris Controls (the erstwhile 'GE Harris' and now within corporate GE Transportation); to Dean Scott Mitchell, Dick Fisher, Don Selby and Ralph Leffingwell (all retired and active at the time of writing); Ian Livingstone (Wabtec); the late John Layton; Mike Korb; Mike Iden (ex-Union Pacific Railroad); Richard L Kimball Jnr (ex-Southern Railway); and various people associated with the Southern Railway Historical Society of Spencer, North Carolina, USA.

I also recognise the many people who submitted associated material and images that may not have made it into the book. I greatly appreciate their time and effort on my behalf. I hope they enjoy this story and I apologise that it took so long.